THE DUFFER'S HANDBOOK OF GOLF

BY
GRANTLAND RICE
AND
CLARE BRIGGS

FOREWORD BY

HERBERT WARREN WIND

AFTERWORD BY

JIM MURRAY

CLASSICS OF GOLF
EDITION

STAMFORD, CONNECTICUT

Foreword

In the 1920s, after the First World War had been success-fully concluded, life in the United States changed radically. In their search for a more fruitful use of their free time, two million Americans became golfers, and what had been a small game, played almost exclusively by the upper class, became for the first time a part of the fabric of American life. If any single book signified the coming of age of golf in the United States, it was "The Duffer's Handbook of Golf". Published in 1926, it was the joint work of Grantland Rice, the most admired sportswriter in the country, and Clare Briggs, the gifted cartoonist, who was perhaps best known for his nationally syndicated comic strip, "Mr. and Mrs.". Cre-ative persons are supposed to recognize changes in the na-tional psyche earlier than the man on the street. In the case of "The Duffer's Handbook of Golf," this was certainly true. It was nothing less than a celebration of golf, that all too absorbing game that borders on being a way of life.

Grantland Rice, a man of unusual talent and character, was born in Murfreesboro, Tennessee, in 1880. He graduated from Vanderbilt University, where he played football and baseball, in 1901. He joined the Nashville Daily News *that year. In those days it was not uncommon for newspapermen to change papers at fairly frequent intervals. Rice went on to the Atlanta* Journal *in 1902, to the Nashville* Tennesseean *in 1906, to the New York* Evening Mail *in 1911, and to the New York* Tribune *in 1914. He had taken up golf at thirty and became a low-handicap player with a good deal of knowledge of the game's technique. This undoubtedly accounted for his being the first important sportswriter who viewed golf as a* major sport. He covered the top tournaments with the same vigor he devoted to baseball, college football, horse racing, and boxing —the big sports of that era. The Tribune Syndicate arranged in 1930 for Rice's daily column, "The Sportlight" to be run in newspapers from coast to coast. In the 1930s and 1940s, when it was standard practice for many movie theatres to back up the feature picture with a newsreel and assorted short subjects, Rice helped to produce and narrated a series of one-reel films called Grantland Rice's Sportlight. There were times when Rice was so busy that Ted Husing, the radio sports announcer, had to be called in to do the narration.

Rice met Bobby Jones when the latter was just a young man of enormous talent. They became fast friends. After Jones finally broke through by winning our national Open at the Inwood Country Club, on Long Island, in 1923, his Boswell, O.B. Keeler of the Atlanta Journal, was on hand at every championship he played here and in Great Britain to report his many thrilling triumphs. Rice was also present on most of those occasions. Millions of Americans got to know Jones through Rice's newspaper columns and through the articles on Jones written by Keeler, Rice, and Bernard Darwin, for The American Golfer, a handsome, tasteful, monthly magazine published by Conde Nast. Blessed with the perfect managing editor in Innis Brown, Rice was somehow able to find the time to serve as the editor of The American Golfer from 1920 to 1936, when the magazine stopped publication, a victim of the Depression. Jones, after his retirement from competitive golf following his Grand Slam in 1930, founded the Augusta National Golf Club, in Augusta, Georgia, and co-designed its splendid course with Alister MacKenzie. Rice was a charter member of the club. In his pleasant, clear-headed way, he contributed a valuable sense of perspective during the club's formative years. In 1934, the first year that Augusta National's Invitational Tournament was held, Rice took to calling it the Masters in his articles. A few years later, when everybody was referring to the tournament as the Masters, Jones, who had not wished to seem immodest, agreed to let the tournament he hosted be officially known as the Masters.

Grantland Rice—"Granny" to his many friends—stayed at the forefront of the sports world until he was well into his seventies. In 1953, when Ben Hogan was welcomed home after his victory in the British Open, at Carnoustie, with a ticker-tape parade down the canyons of lower Broadway, there was no question that Grantland Rice was the proper man to serve as the toastmaster at the luncheon held at Toot Shor's restaurant. Rice provided just the right note on that memorable occasion.

Clare Briggs was born in Reedsburg, Wisconsin, in 1895. After spending two years at the University of Nebraska, he went to work as an illustrator for the St. Louis Globe Democrat. His peregrinations took him to the New York World, the Chicago Tribune, and then to the New York Tribune Syndicate in 1914. He had a remarkable talent for capturing many of the recognizable types in the American scene and presenting their preoccupations, moods, hopes, letdowns, moments of elation, puzzlements, and needs as they mixed with their families and friends. He put the idioms of the day in their mouths, and his men and women came right off the page full of life. Along with the "Mr. and Mrs." comic strip, he was renowned for his series of one-panel drawings which elaborated humorously on such themes as "How To Start the Day Wrong," "When a Feller Needs a Friend," "Someone Is Always Taking the Joy out of Life," and "What a Grand and Glorious Feeling!". Briggs played his golf at the Wykagyl Country Club, in New Rochelle, Westchester. I don't believe that any other comic artist has caught so memorably the assorted characters that peopled golf in the 1920s and still do today. Many of Clare Briggs's originals hang on the walls at Wykagyl.

"The Duffer's Handbook of Golf" is made up in equal parts of Briggs's cartoons and Rice's writing. Rice knew all the leading golfers, and he includes tips from such champions as Walter Hagen, Jim Barnes, Chick Evans, and Bobby Jones. He understood the workings of the golf swing extremely well, and the reader is in very good hands when Rice leads him through such phases of the game as On Steering the Ball, How To Lose Distance, Beyond the Pin, On Hooking the Ball, About the Two Hands, On Sinking the Putt, The Ideal Golf Temperament, and Then There's the Spoon. Rice was a lifelong enthusiast of stirring, romantic ballads and other verse, and he also provides his golf-oriented versions of familiar poems by Coleridge, Longfellow, Stevenson, and Kipling.

When I was growing up, "The Duffer's Handbook of Golf" was one of the two golf books in my family's library. (The other was Bobby Jones's "Down the Fairway.") Its appeal seems evergreen to me, and I hope that this proves to be true for you.

Jim Murray, the celebrated sports columnist of the Los Angeles Times *and the syndicated papers of the Times-Mirror company, has been one of America's most popular sportswriters since the 1950s. A graduate of Trinity College in Hartford, Connecticut, he became a member of the Los Angeles bureau of Time, Inc. When* Sports Illustrated *was inaugurated in 1954, Murray's lively reports on the sports scene on the West Coast became one of S.I.'s standard features. Later lured away by the Los Angeles* Times, *Murray has continued over the decades to provide his millions of readers with his witty and shrewd observations on the world of sport.*

Herbert Warren Wind

THE DUFFER'S
HANDBOOK OF GOLF

THE MACMILLAN COMPANY
NEW YORK · BOSTON · CHICAGO · DALLAS
ATLANTA · SAN FRANCISCO

MACMILLAN & CO., LIMITED
LONDON · BOMBAY · CALCUTTA
MELBOURNE

THE MACMILLAN CO. OF CANADA, LTD.
TORONTO

THE DUFFER'S
HANDBOOK
of
GOLF

By *Grantland Rice and Clare Briggs*

NEW YORK · THE MACMILLAN COMPANY · MCMXXVI

PRINTED IN THE UNITED STATES OF AMERICA
BY THE BERWICK AND SMITH COMPANY

CONTENTS

Contents

Contents

THE DUFFER'S
HANDBOOK OF GOLF

What Golf Is

GOLF is, in part, a game; but only in part. It is also in part a religion, a fever, a vice, a mirage, a frenzy, a fear, an abscess, a joy, a thrill, a pest, a disease, an uplift, a brooding melancholy, a dream of yesterday, a disappointing to-day and a hope for to-morrow.

"Hope deferred maketh the heart sick," and golf is hope deferred. Golf is light on the hills and a shadow in the valley. It is the first whisper of the trees in early spring. And late in the fall it is the gaunt spectre of leafless oaks that stand stark against a coming winter sky.

It is the song of streams and the lash of surf against the shore.

It is the strong wine that looseneth all tongues and starts a babble longer and louder than Babel ever knew.

It is philosophy making a losing fight, ambition shattered and the eternal ego held in bitter bounds.

It is also philosophy triumphant just often enough to show that miracles can happen.

Golf is everything that represents outdoors—trees, rivers, lakes, hills, valleys, ponds, sky, turf, surf, rain, sun, wind, sand and grass through mile after mile.

There may be few who can see any beauty around except that of a well-hit shot or a lucky bound, but it is at least there for them to see in case the grip of the ancient game can be broken only for the moment.

Golf is companionship and feud, friendliness and fury, ambition and despair. It is concentration, disintegration, inflammation, elation and desperation.

In short it is the Soul of the Race with the cover taken off.

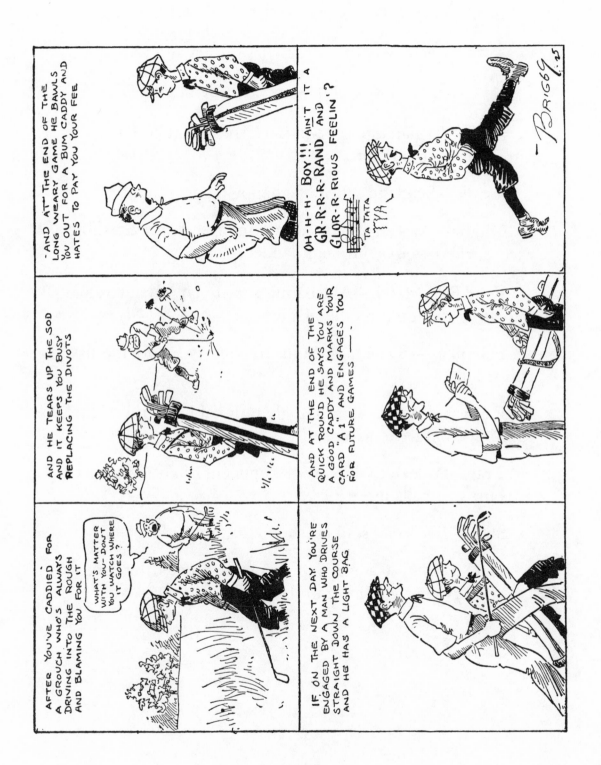

A Few Definitions

THE easiest shot in golf—any conceded putt.

Alibi—Explanations of perfect shots that just carried into some deep bunker.

Stymie—Scotland's idea of a happy moment in life.

Caddie—Any small boy keenly interested in everything except where your wild hook landed.

Four-Ball Match—A debating society largely interested in getting the jump on the first tee.

Handicap—Something to insure victory before the first ball is hit.

Fairway—A green but largely uninhabited strip of turf running from tee to green.

Trap—A device which your opponent's ball jumps over as yours just rolls in.

Slice—The great soul crusher of all time.

Heel Print—A small depression designated by fate to catch every shot you hit into the sand.

A Few Definitions

Green—A smooth surface largely given over to the habit of taking putts.

Short Putt—Any putt you miss.

Lucky Gobble—Any putt your opponent holes.

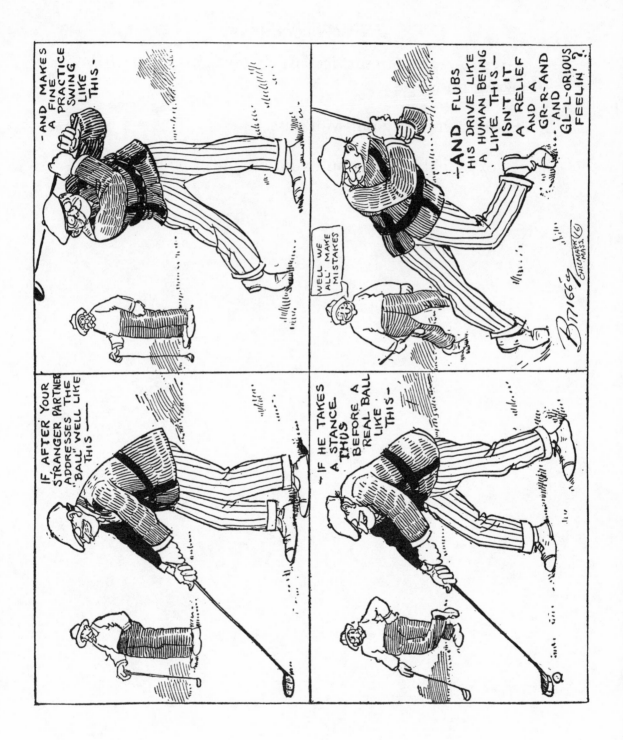

Get the Habit

HABIT is one of the directing forces of life. Also of golf, a subdivision of life. So the main idea is to work on the right habit.

Here are a few Habit Suggestions:

1. Make a habit of using a lighter grip and lack of hurry for all short putts.

2. Make a habit of hitting all approach putts up to or past the cup.

3. Develop the habit of a smooth, even back swing. Practice it. Think about it.

4. Make a habit of NOT pressing, of NOT trying too hard, of NOT thinking in terms of extra effort or over-effort. Make a habit of natural effort.

5. Develop the habit of thinking about hitting the ball, and not where the ball may be going.

The Mental Side

THE mental side of golf is a peculiar animal. It is vastly important; yet it is not based upon intellectuality or imagination. Any thinking which takes place must in no sense be fancy. It must be without any frills. The mental side, as Jim Barnes puts it, "is thinking of the right thing at the right time," and not thinking of anything else.

The four controlling qualities are Serenity, Determination, Relaxation and Concentration.

A relaxed mental state means relaxed nerves and relaxed muscles. There should be the elimination of all outside thought except hitting the ball in a natural, comfortable way.

Once the stance is taken the remainder of the swing should be left to the subconscious mind, the instinct or muscle memory. See that the grip isn't too tight and that the back swing starts smoothly. Then forget everything you ever knew or heard of.

If the swing is wrong and you haven't practiced, nothing will help, anyway.

If the swing is sound in the few important details, do your thinking before you take your stance, and from that point on let muscle memory take control.

Concentration means the elimination of all outside

factors, grip, stance, pivoting, bunkers—all except hitting the ball. A fairly blank mind, after the back swing has started, is a great help.

If you are thinking only of hitting the ball, and not of grip, stance, pivot, the bunker or the pond to be carried, the chances are you will look at the ball, keep your head still and swing on through. And that is the major part of golf.

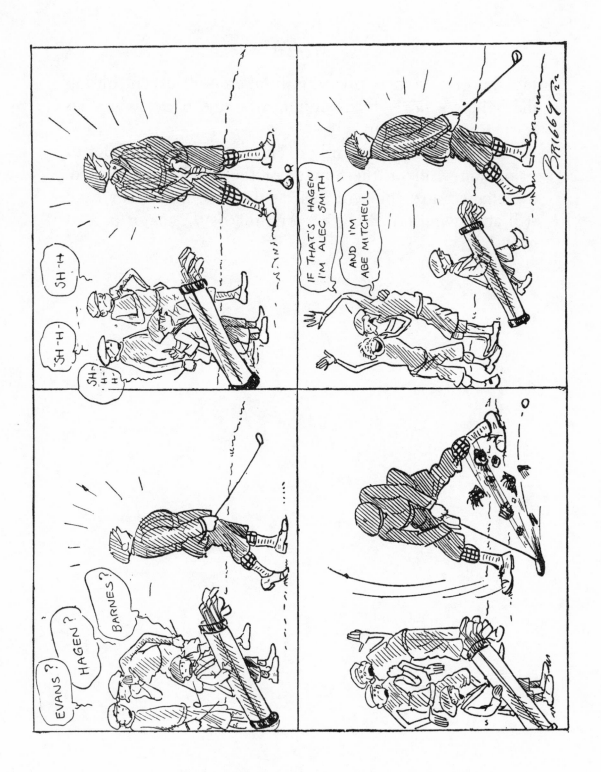

Songs of Dufferdom

THE friendly pit, so full of sand,
   I love through May and June;
I take a niblick in my hand
And spend the afternoon.

The fairway's green and long and wide
   Where one can play with par;
And yet somehow I'd rather hide
   Down where the heel prints are.

Though others scorn its sandy showers
   Or turn from it and flee,
I've spent so many, many hours
   That it's like home to me.

The Caddie's Place

AN extremely nervous, fidgety and jumpy golfer had a three-foot putt to sink.

"Boy," he said to his caddie, "you'll move sure just as I am putting, so I want you to go over and hide back of that mound."

The caddie hid back of the mound, completely removed from sight.

The nervous golfer, after keying his system up to the cracking point, jabbed at the ball and missed.

"I knew it," he yelled to the caddie still hidden, "I knew it—you must have moved!"

Which is a fair sample of all the golfing alibis heaped upon the caddie's slender back.

He usually has enough to do in the way of carrying twice as many clubs as any golfer ever needs without having all the sins of dufferdom and stardom heaped upon him.

A caddie, as a rule, is about as good a caddie as the disposition of his employer.

The good sport usually has a good caddie. The bum sport never has. We have seen irascible golfing types who could wreck the best caddie in the world by the third hole.

Any golfer who has from ten to sixteen clubs in his bag has already given the caddie all he can do without expecting him to find balls lost in impenetrable thickets.

The caddie makes no pretense at being a combination superman, truck horse, magician, guide, bloodhound and teacher. Yet that is what about 500,000 golfers expect him to be. And when he falls down on part of this combination their lamentations and execrations rock the reverberating hills.

There are of course some caddies addicted to the subtle art of hiccoughing just as one is driving or putting. In that case take the club you need and wave him politely out of range.

The golfer as a rule gets as good a caddie as he deserves to get. Most of the time even better.

There are ten times as many bad golfers as there are bad caddies.

The caddie is the camel of golf. You know how much fun the game would be if his tribe suddenly became extinct. He's a pretty useful institution to conserve, protect and develop.

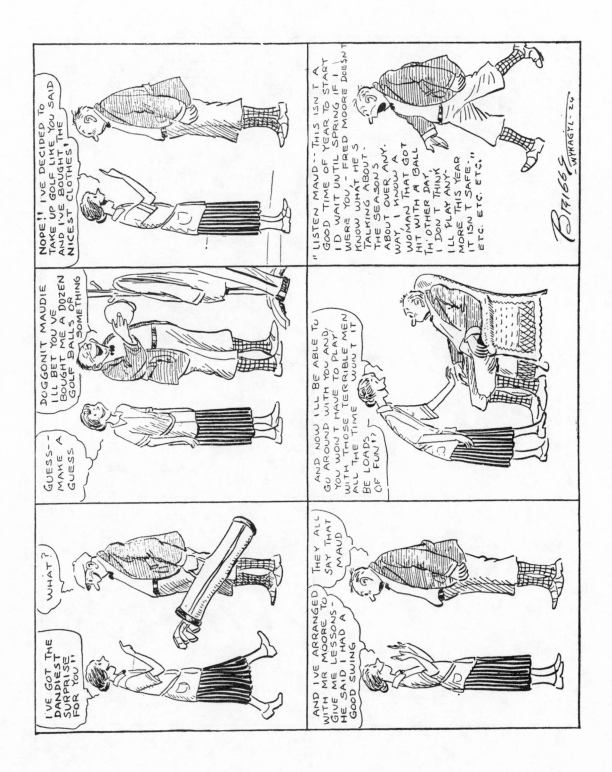

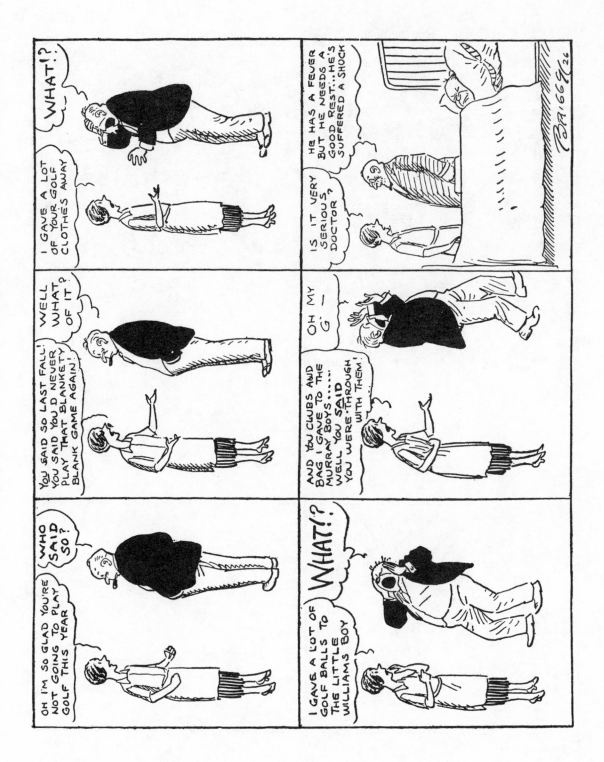

When to Hit

ACCORDING to Bill Tilden the great mistake most young tennis players make is waiting a trifle too long and then rushing things too much at the finish.

The idea is to start in a hurry, get there in time and so be set for the stroke.

Most golfers have a double fault when it comes to hitting. They hurry the back swing and they hurry the down swing. They are so keen to hit the ball that few of them can wait. The result is they start the down swing before the back swing is finished, and then, applying the punch too quickly, tighten up and check the club head on its way through.

First of all, the back swing must be completed. One thing at a time. When the back swing is finished the down swing must start smoothly, without being rushed. Don't be in any hurry to apply the snap or punch. If you keep the club head increasing its speed on through the ball there is no need of trying to apply any sudden power.

The swing that you take at a cigar stump or dandelion head is usually the right one because you haven't killed all the flexibility in your wrists and arms by hitting too quickly. Attempting to apply extra power simply means tightening the muscular system to the complete destruction of timing, rhythm, smoothness and a cheerful result.

What About Your Grip?

THE golf grip is hardly to be listed as one of the most important episodes of existence.

In many ways it is hardly a golf essential, despite all the chatter you may hear about it.

John Ball and Jerry Travers used the old-fashioned, non-lapping V-grip, and between them they won twelve amateur championships and two or three open championships of America and Great Britain.

Bobby Jones and Walter Hagen have the overlapping grip while Francis Ouimet and Gene Sarazen have the interlocking, where the little finger of the right hand is intertwined with the forefinger of the left.

Abe Mitchell drives with the straight V-grip and plays his irons with the overlapping.

So don't let the grip worry you into any illness.

But you might remember these few details—viz.:

When the left hand is well over and the right hand under you will be more inclined to hook.

When the left hand is more to the left side of the club shaft and the right hand is over you will be more likely to slice. It is usually safer to keep the left hand fairly well over the club.

It isn't a bad idea to have the two Vs formed by the thumb and forefinger both pointing to the right shoulder, or thereabouts. That at least is a fairly safe grip to work with.

The Golfer's Dirge

I'VE licked them with their aching heads
   That throbbed in every pore;
I've licked them when they hadn't slept
A wink the night before;
I've licked them with lumbago,
And I've licked them with the grip,
I've licked them when their insteps hurt
And when they had the pip;
I've licked them with the fever
And I've licked them with the ague,
I've licked them when their feet were sore
And when they had the plague;
I've licked them when the skin was off
With blisters on their hands,
I've licked them when their aching backs
Were full of mustard bands;
I've licked them when their knees were stiff
And necks with boils were rife,
      But—
I never licked a well man in my life.

What About the Two Hands?

TENNIS, polo and squash are three of the more important games where only one hand is employed in making the stroke.

Baseball and golf are the two leading games where both hands enter the action.

The main trouble in golf is getting the two hands to work with any team play. Often they don't speak. The left hand frequently doesn't know what the right hand is thinking about.

The right hand, usually being the stronger member, wants to take control. This is wrong.

At the start of the swing the left hand should have the firmer grip and the left hand, wrist and arm should have control of the back swing.

They all work together with the turn of the left shoulder and the left knee.

They are still in control, left hand, wrist and arm, as the down swing starts.

The right hand will be fairly itching to get in and take control, but make it wait a while.

At the right moment, not too soon, near the finish of the swing, the right hand finally leaps into command and whips the club head through. When this takes place there must be a firm left hand, a firm left wrist and a firm left leg to hit against.

The right hand hitting against a firm left hand and a firm left wrist develops the "whip," "snap" or greater club-head speed that is needed.

Don't let the right hand take control too quickly. Don't let the left hand and wrist ever get limp or flabby through any part of the swing.

The Most Important Stroke

YOU hear a lot about the most important stroke in golf. Drive—approach—putt—what not.

Don't let them kid you. Kidding duffers is one of the great industries of the age.

There is only one important stroke in golf. There is only one stroke you must think about, consider, ponder over and plan to the absolute elimination of everything else. It is the only stroke that matters a half whoop in Heligoland—and that is——

The next stroke you have to play.

The rest of it is nothing, as sounding brass and tinkling cymbal.

Froth—seaweed—ashes—wind-blown dust.

It all comes down to one important moment—the next stroke you have to play.

Give that your polite attention and make 'em laugh it off.

Short Approaches

HELL hath no fury like a bunkered dub.

It is better to live with a brawling woman in a narrow house than a duffer off his game.

If at first you don't succeed, try looking at the ball.

The paths of glory lead but to the heel print.

Unfortunately no golf scientist has yet invented an interlocking tongue.

It is much simpler and easier to hit the back of the cup on the 19th hole.

Eat, drink and be merry, for to-morrow you may be off your game again.

He who swings and lifts his head will say things better left unsaid.

It's a poor rule that doesn't work your way.

The art of self-defense—a pair of ear muffs for the locker room.

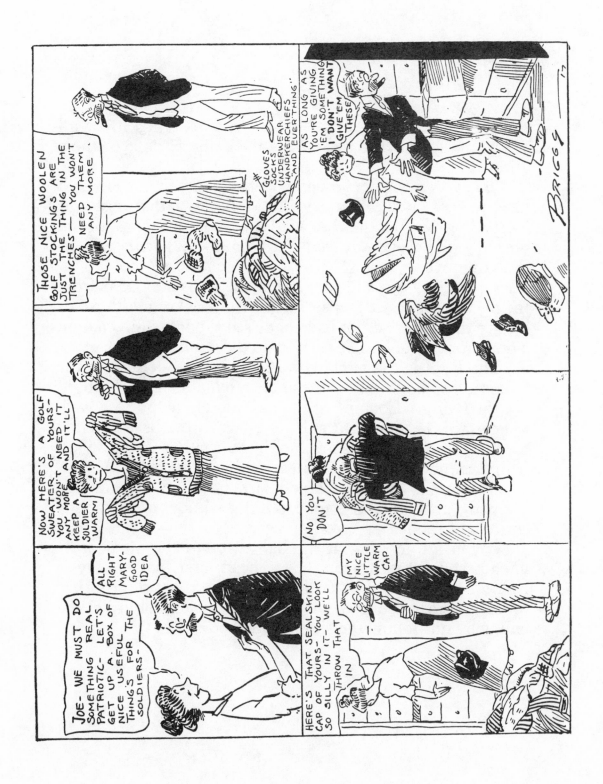

On Looking at the Ball

A TRICK golfer played five or six strokes in a row with his eyes turned away from the ball. He played them all well.

"That shows," remarked an observer, "that you don't have to look at the ball. I always thought that idea was mostly bunk." But the observer failed to notice that the trick golfer, with his eyes turned away from the ball, still held his head unmoved.

The main object in looking at the ball is to keep from lifting the head. It is also intended to make one think of hitting the ball, and not have harassed thoughts directed on a bunker or a pond to be carried on the stroke at hand.

The head is the anchor to the swing. Looking at the ball is not so important if the anchor remains fixed throughout the swing. Looking at the ball merely helps, in a way, to keep this head anchor still. For when the head is lifted the body and the hands are lifted, the rhythm of the swing is broken and the stroke is nearly always spoiled.

An acrobat might be able to lift his head without lifting body, arms and the stroke, but not without a neck made entirely of rubber.

If you are looking at the ball through the moment of impact you are not lifting your head, and that is why it isn't a bad idea to look at the target you are trying to hit. Since it is easier to keep the head still while looking at the ball, why not follow the simpler method?

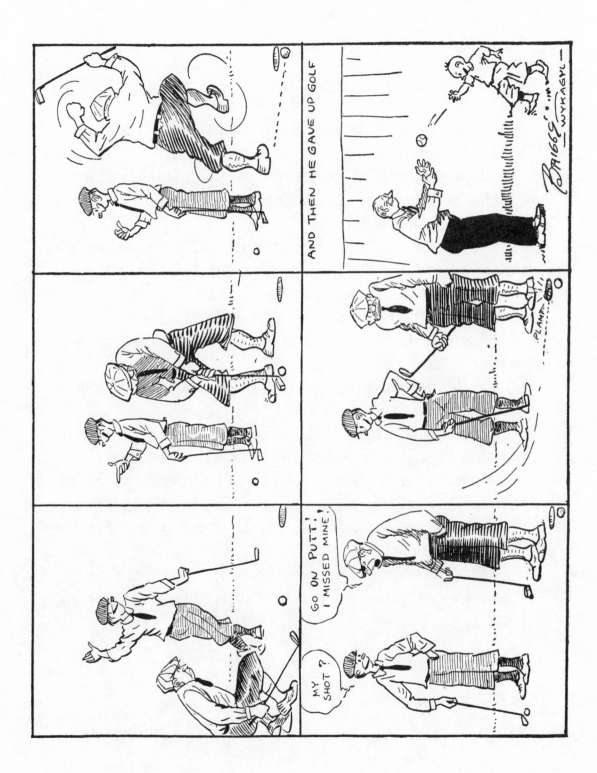

The Use of Balance

ABOUT one party in a million can hit with any force when off balance.

About two million golfers try to—with wan success.

One of the main features of balance is correct use or transference of weight.

On the back swing as the left knee and left shoulder are turned in, or pivoted, most of the weight is naturally thrown to the right foot and the right leg.

Anyway about 60 or 70 percent of the weight is.

Now comes the main problem, the tug of war, the seat of the trouble.

On the down swing about 99 golfers out of every hundred do one of two things—

They either throw their weight forward too soon or else they hit with the weight still upon the right leg.

What they should do is to let the weight come to the left foot and the left leg as the down swing starts, and so use the left leg as a guidepost and a shock point for the moment of impact.

The right side and shoulder can follow up the swing if this is done with the balance held intact by the supporting left leg.

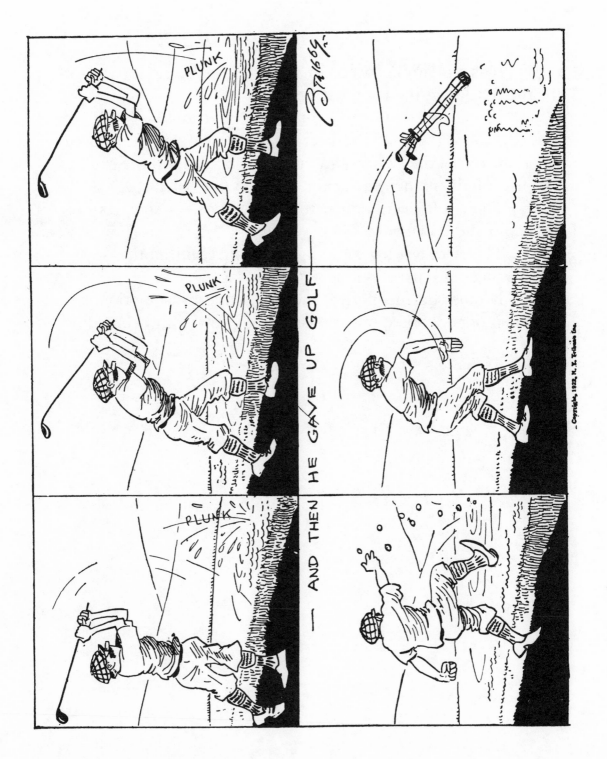

It is no simple problem to get this weight forward to the left leg at the right moment.

If you follow Hagen, Jones and Macdonald Smith you will know that the left heel is fairly well off the ground at the top of the swing—and that it is back upon the ground just a half moment after the down swing is started.

Their left heels return to earth almost as soon as they begin the downward blow.

This firm left leg to hit against helps both in the way of distance and direction.

It must be instinctive and automatic as a motion, but when once worked out it means both power and control.

Fable

ONCE upon a time a certain golfer met another golfer and without any undue waste of time proceeded to describe every stroke played on the round just completed.

He exuded intimate details of the snappy mashie approach which would have finished stone dead on the first green if it hadn't thumped into a guarding pit.

He spoke feelingly of the perfect brassie shot on the third which unfortunately hit a tree and caromed out of bounds.

[31]

Then there was the flawless iron shot on the fifth which finished up in an unplayable lie back of the barn.

It was a vivid episode from beginning to end. The second golfer tilted an interested ear to catch every word, without making any move to start a description of his own.

He followed the narrative word for word without practicing any quick starts for a getaway.

MORAL—There is no type of miracle that can't happen at least once in golf.

Just Here and There

GOLF," remarked one pro. quite solemnly, "is all in the fingers. They must have the feel, the touch, the control. When they have, the game is simple." Once in a while.

"Golf," remarked another sage pro., "is just one thing—Rhythm. That's all. Rhythm is based on relaxation, on lack of over-trying. It is just a simple, natural, unhurried swing or swipe. It's the basis of the golf swing. And it isn't hard to get, if one will concentrate on rhythm above everything else." So we've heard.

Whereupon a third esteemed pro. had his say: "There are just five words that tell the story of golf—Keep Back Of The Ball. If you keep back of the ball you have something to hit with. But 98 percent manage to sway forward just as they are hitting. They are not balanced to hit anything hard enough to knock it a foot. Keep back of the ball and the rest is easy."

Finger touch—Rhythm—Keep back of the ball——Sounds almost too simple to bother about. Still, let's give it a try.

Something to Think Over

I FOLLOWED Chick Evans once through a round in an amateur championship where almost every iron shot he hit flew straight for the pin.

A slight drizzle was falling and there were intermittent gusts of wind, hardly calculated to help one's play.

But Evans on this occasion furnished one of the finest iron-play exhibitions any one ever watched.

His timing was faultless. There was a perfect combination of flexibility and rhythm to his play worth a long trip to see.

There was no hurry, no sudden hitting, no quick tightening of the muscles.

There was almost no effort of any sort.

Later on we talked the round over. "I am quite sure," he said, "that I gripped the shaft lighter or softer to-day than I ever did before. I made no attempt to tighten up. So I could feel the play of the club head and a lot of elasticity in my wrists. This kept me from hurrying either the back swing or the down swing and it gave the club blade its chance to speed through in a natural way."

Which is something every golfer might think over.

The Lone Kick

I DO not mind the sloping green,
The pits that wind and creep;
I like the bunker's noble mien,
Though heel prints there are deep.

The Lone Kick

I do not mind the mutt who talks
Just as I swing away,
I do not curse the hick who stalks
In line just as I play.

My temper's soft by green and tee
Though winter winds may blow;
There isn't much that bothers me
No matter where I go.

But where I burn is when some dub
Whose game is none too strong,
Horns in each time I fluff or flub
To tell me what was wrong.

Missing Ingredients

DUE largely to the existence of human nature in bulk, 98 percent of all who play golf will remain in the duffer class, which is somewhere beyond 100 for the round.

There are many reasons for this dip into depression.

In the first place the average human being lacks the patience needed to practice the right way of swinging long enough to have it become instinct or second nature.

In the second place the average human isn't overburdened with the gift of concentration upon the one vital thing to do at the moment.

In the third place the average human being isn't afflicted with too much natural rhythm. It is his nature to employ effort where ease is required.

In the fourth place the average human has given almost no attention to the matter of mental control, which in golf should be an absence of conscious thinking as the stroke is played.

The average human being is still wondering, as he hits his putt, what the right line is and how hard he should hit. He is still wondering, as he plays his approach, whether he can carry that bunker or whether he is using the right club.

There are few who can make definite decisions in

advance and eliminate all other details except the matter of hitting the ball.

The first weakness, named lack of patience for practice, is of course the main collapse of the golfing tribe.

Small boys of 12 and 13 have proved through practice they could break 80. Men beyond 50, starting golf late in life, have proved through practice they could break 85.

Girls of 15 and women of 65 have done better than 83. Through practice. But patience is not one of the overflowing or abundant human virtues.

And patience is needed to practice hour after hour through week after week until the swing finally becomes largely a matter of muscle memory.

Golf will always be a tangle for the average golfer because his swing is largely a matter of conscious thought, or conscious effort, rather than the building of right habits which operate instinctively.

The golf swing must first be learned and then it must be forgotten so it can work in a mechanical way.

But it can't be learned by the absence treatment. There are only a few essential things to learn—balance and timing being the most important—but they come over no easy trail. They are the products of patience and perseverance, two ingredients which are none too plentiful.

To reach this improvement the golfer must practice the

mental side as well as the physical. He must practice the matter of mental relaxation as well as physical. He must practice the habit of making up his mind in advance as to the type of stroke to play, and then forget everything else.

Mainly he must practice enough to have a fair mechanical foundation to work and to have a share of confidence at least in his ability to hit a drive, play an approach or make a putt.

The average golfer would rather play above 100 than face what he thinks is the drudgery of practice. So he will keep on playing above 100 save upon the rare occasions where something snaps, everything works in the right way, and he finds a 94 upon his card. But this will not happen often enough to make any dent in his grand average total around 105.

The Crafty Art of Slicing

"OH WHAT A PRETTY SLICE"

THERE are twenty-five or thirty ways of developing a slice if one happens to be in the mood. There are just as many ways of slicing if one doesn't happen to be in the mood. With so many different methods at hand, slicing is one of the simplest of all the golfing arts. Almost any duffer can do it. Almost every duffer does.

The Crafty Art of Slicing

You must be sure of course to drag the club head across the ball at the moment of impact to have the perfect slice that spirals away into the woods, out of bounds or the rough. Or possibly a pond, lake or bunker. Perhaps back of a tree.

If you have an uncontrollable desire to slice, the surest method is to start the club head back on a line outside of the ball, outside of the line of flight. Also bring the club head down on this same outside line. Don't start the club head back on an inside arc, swinging through from the inside out. This may cause a hook or a straight ball. Another sound slicing method is to aim to the left of the course, allowing for a slice, and then let the hands and body get well in front of the club head at the moment of impact. This method rarely fails. Gripping tightly with the right hand on the back swing and lifting the club head abruptly is one of the surest of the slicing aids. It rarely fails one time out of ten.

A fairly sure way of slicing is to stand too far away from the ball so you will have to fall or lean forward to hit it. Which you will do with the heel of the club. There is still another simple method of meeting this problem. Sway to the right and throw all the weight on the right foot and right leg. Then start for the deep rough or the thicket on the right side of the course; for that is where the ball will be.

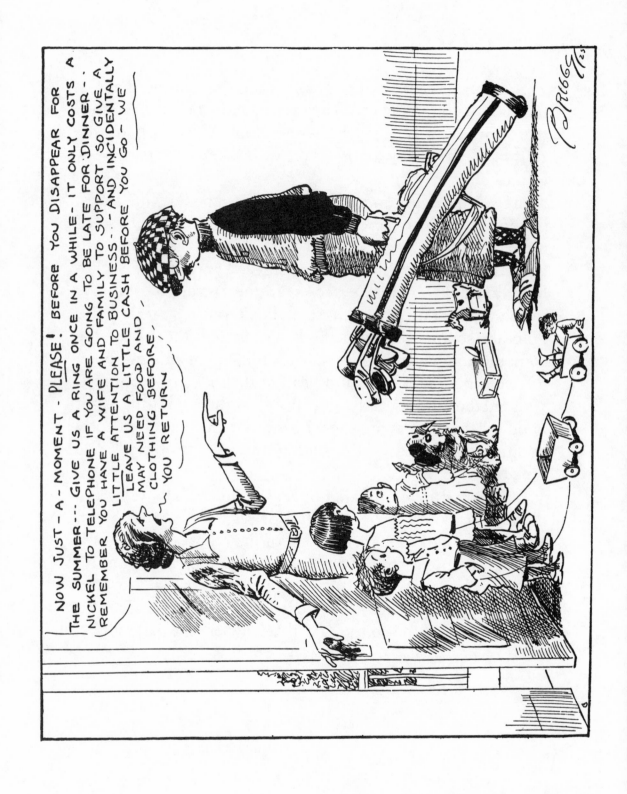

On Steering the Ball

STANDING on the tee there is a flank of woods to the right of the course.

To the left there are sand-filled abysses of woe and trouble.

Facing this combination the average golfer no longer steps up and swings with anything approaching carefree abandon.

His main effort is to steer the ball. And it has been proved by scientific research that no golfer is equipped with any of the devices which make up a steering gear.

Steering the ball is next to an impossibility. It has cost as much strokes and as much painful melancholy on a golf course as any other single blight.

The idea is to play the shot—to hit the ball. Even that could be easier on off days.

When the steering problem is added there will be nothing but débris left.

How to Talk Golf

THERE are two classes to deal with in this widespread and well-known art.

The prospective victim may be either a golfer or a non-golfer.

If he or she is a non-golfer the first move to make is to

carefully and craftily herd him or her into a corner where there is no possible chance of escape.

It is just as well, of course, to see that the victim isn't armed.

Once the victim is securely herded, he is then like a trout that is hooked. You can describe every stroke at your leisure, pausing only to block his frantic efforts at escape.

If the prospective for whom you intend to describe your entire round is another golfer, it is largely a matter of getting the jump.

If you don't beat him to it he will be in there first with his own stirring story of what happened to him, in which case your afternoon or evening will be a total loss.

Once your victim is hooked, don't forget to allude at length to every detail of the round, not forgetting all the perfect shots that unluckily flew out of bounds, flopped into heel prints or came to rest back of trees.

It doesn't make the slightest difference what you say, because he won't be listening anyway.

A Few Words on the Wrist

YOU will hear, at various times, a lot of sage and otherwise debate about the correct uses of the wrists.

Profound words will be spoken on pronating the wrists, breaking the wrists, cocking the wrists and what-notting the wrists, especially what-notting.

Our somewhat dilapidated advice is to think about wrist action and wrist duties just as little as you can, and perhaps still less.

Thoughts concentrated on the wrists and their various duties can tie you into more knots, mental and physical, than a dozen sailors.

When you have taken the club head back as far as you want it to go with a fairly straight and firm left arm, keep the left wrist firm but let it bend or break or give in an easy, natural way at the finish of the back swing.

It will do this anyway if you let it alone. But don't think too much about it. And there is almost no "give" or "break" until the top of the back swing is reached.

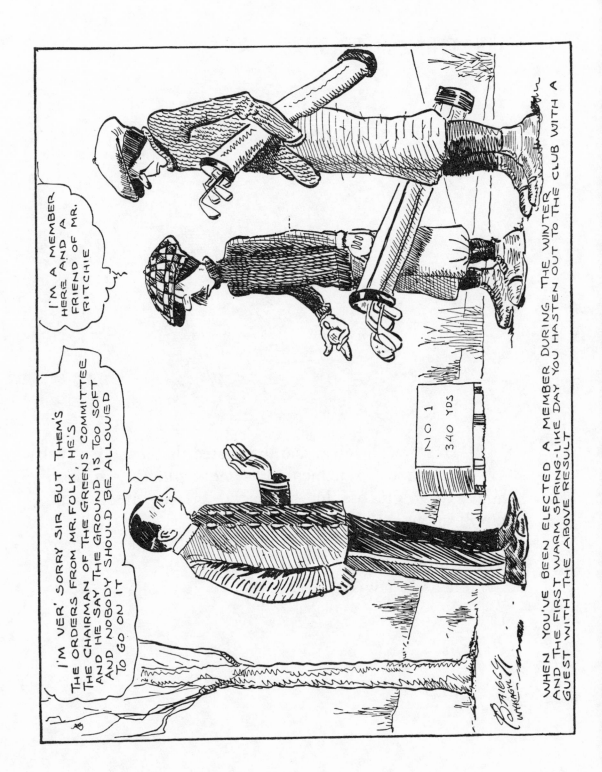

The Glucose Handicap

SOME expert medical man has stated that a sudden rush of anger or excitement puts more glucose, or something akin to glucose, into the blood, thereby precipitating complications.

This can happen in golf about as often as any game in the world.

Here are a few samples.

The Glucose Handicap

Standing on the tee you hit too much under the ball, cut or slice it a trifle, fail to get in the punch and watch the demon sphere float about 147 yards down the middle.

"Good shot," says your opponent, just as you are thinking how terrible it was.

Possibly he means "good shot" for you, comparatively speaking. But all you can do is stand and glare.

Or in the midst of a tight, hectic match you hook one into an impenetrable thicket.

You see the flood of relief cross your opponent's drawn face as he remarks, "Tough luck. I'm sorry."

Knowing just how sorry he is, once more the glucose begins to coagulate in large chunks through your burning veins that may burst into flames at any moment.

The Fairest Flower

INTO the woods the duffer sliced
  Where the May blooms covered all;
Into the woods the duffer went
To find the doggone ball.

The Fairest Flower

He stepped on tender violets
And swore till he was blue;
He scattered daffodils about
And cursed their golden hue.

He stormed and tore up buttercups,
He jerked rare vines apart,
He peered through greens and reds and pinks
But with a sodden heart.

And then with one wild yell of joy
Beyond all price or cost,
He saw the flower of the flock,
The battered ball he'd lost.

The Safer Way

AS between two evils, where the average golfer is concerned, it is better to hit hard than spare the wallop.

Suppose, for example, you come to a range that is a trifle short for your full mashie effort and a trifle long for your mashie niblick. There are experts who will tell you to take the mashie and not swing back so far. Also not to hit quite so lustily.

This is ideal advice, perhaps, for the crack. But not for one of the two million.

If you are under pressure it is easier and simpler and more natural to use the club that calls for the unrepressed swing.

For when you are under pressure the hardest stroke in golf is the spared or softened or shortened blow, an undertaking which calls for complete mental and physical control. To say nothing of more expertness than most golfers have.

This doesn't mean that one should make the mistake of using a mashie where a jigger or mashie iron is needed.

There is no use in lunging your soul out with a mashie, when a firm punch with the longer club will get there more comfortably. Just be wary of too much suppression where you can take another club and hit with greater firmness, not to say abandon.

[55]

Now, About the Drive

IN the first place, get a brassie in place of a driver. The brassie has slightly more loft, is simpler to handle because of this, and gets just about as far.

In the second place, for the grand or general average use a square stance where your feet are on a line parallel to the line of flight.

Get comfortable, or as comfortable as you can. The golfer is supposed to be a human being, not a tree stump or a telegraph post.

Never mind about hitting it a mile. If you do, you won't.

The start is mainly a left-sided proposition. The left hand and wrist are in control and as they start the club head the left shoulder and left knee turn to the right, and don't be afraid to let them turn. It is this pivot which gives the small man or the slight girl a chance for distance.

Let the club head start back smoothly on an arc inside the ball. Don't lift with the right hand.

The left arm, as you have heard before, must be firm and fairly straight. At the top of the swing about 60 percent of the weight is on the right foot and about 40 percent on the ball of the left.

Practice the right swing, the right pivot, the right everything in your room, on the tee, anywhere and everywhere you can until it feels natural and instinctive. Otherwise you might as well be plowing or heaving bricks.

Finish the back swing first, and then let the down swing start naturally without any sudden lurch or swish. Give the club head its way and let it gather speed on through the ball. All this while the left hand, the left wrist and the left arm are firm, never loose and flabby. The right will usually take up its job soon enough without being hurried into action.

Just try to be natural without trying to do too much. You might be surprised. On the down swing let the club head come on the ball as if you were trying to hit a trifle to the right. The line of the club head is from the inside out.

Once the back swing has started there should be just one idea left—Hit the ball. Which is about all there is to it.

The Favorite Weapon

THE pet club in your golfing kit can have its disadvantages, as well as its sunny side.

It can curse as well as bless.

It may be an old warped driver, an old spoon, an old iron or an old mashie. For some reason it has become a stand-by in time of storm and trouble. It has become the lone port in a gale.

I have seen golfers play a spoon for distances around 100 or 120 yards because the spoon was a pet and the mashie was an abomination. They had confidence in the spoon and a deep-seated loathing, dread and terror of the mashie.

The pet club is an old friend, but there is usually no distinct reason why it ever became a pet. Friendship isn't based on reason, anyway.

Yet this pet club has its weak side. Suddenly in the midst of some hard battle you discover that the pet club is no longer behaving as a pet or a friend should. It throws you down, and then, with your heart full of black bitterness, you know that all is lost and that destruction is only a step away. Life at that moment has little to offer and the future is darker still.

The pet club is a necessary institution. But it must not be catered to out of reason. It must be kept, at least partially, in its place. There are certain large moments when it must be rushed to the rescue of fluttering nerves and fading hopes. But don't let these moments occur too often. Being a slave to a game is one thing. Being a cringing captive to one warped club is something else.

On Looking at the Ball

IN the first place it isn't as important as you might think. Looking at the ball does this much good—it helps to keep the head still and the shoulders in the same, unlifted plane.

And that latter matter is something you have to do—if you care about cracking 125.

It can do this much harm—make you self-conscious, stiff and tied up in mental knots. It can make you concentrate on the ball, in place of the swing. It can help break up rhythm.

It is better to look at the ball, of course. But not to think too much about it.

If the swing is smooth and even and unhurried, you are pretty sure to keep the head still.

And if the head is still you are pretty sure to look at the ball. That's about the way it works.

If you don't hurry the back swing and don't hurry the down swing, it is easy enough to keep the head still and to look at the ball.

If you violate the first principles, all is lost, including honor.

Not looking at the ball usually means lifting the head,

and lifting the head means lifting the shoulders and dis-arranging the swing.

The best way to look at the ball is not to think about anything except hitting it.

And that doesn't mean thinking of the bunker or the lake or the what not that must be carried.

So don't think too much about looking at the ball. When the back swing has started don't think about anything. Let nature and muscle memory take their course.

THERE MUST BE SOMETHING WRONG WITH THIS HOUSE ACCOUNT OF MINE - I CERTAINLY DON T OWE THIS MUCH
HOW BOUT A LITTLE FOUR-HANDED GAME OF STUD OSCAR?
HE'S ALWAYS WANTED THE COURSE TO HIM-SELF - HE'S GOT IT
HE'S HOLLERIN' 'FORE' - I'LL SAY IT'S. THE HEIGHTH OF PRECAUTION
LOOK OUT FOR THAT FOURSOME AHEAD OF YOU FRANK.
FORE
BRIGGS '22

The Duffer's Recompense

THE point has been made that the duffer, playing a course in 127 strokes, gets much more exercise out of the game than a crack player shooting a 71.

The duffer's interest in this recompense seems to be languid, bordering at times on the morbid.

Yet, after a fashion, it is a recompense. And it is not the only one the average golfer has.

Take the case, for example, of Mr. Irvin S. Cobb in playing the Sleepy Hollow course. Many of the other members had been only conscious of a green, narrow fairway with a vague bordering of woods to the right and left.

Against this Mr. Cobb, in the pursuit of golf balls he had struck slightly off the intended line, one day came upon a badger at work.

He was the only one who had ever gone deep enough into the woods to come upon a hedgehog, a muskrat and quantities of wild fauna from one to two miles off the fairway.

He came upon virgin oaks of rare beauty which no one else had looked upon.

Mr. Cobb is quite content to have the others get their "pars" and "birdies." In addition to being a golfer he had also become a naturalist, a geologist and a traveler of note.

Who is there to measure the entire game solely against the par of the course?

How to Make a Hole in 9

WHILE making a hole in 9 is not one of the most difficult of all the golfing arts, it is not as simple as many may think it to be. Yet if one follows instructions carefully it can be accomplished with fair consistency.

The surest way is to miss a short putt on the preceding green and then advance to the next tee thinking about that missed short putt while applying to the game of golf in general every known epithet that one can remember. Continue to brood over that missed putt and to think about it exclusively as you lash at your tee shot with a tight grip and a fast back swing. You will probably drive the first ball out of bounds and top the next attempt into the rough. Then, without calming or soothing your flaming soul, slash away at your recovery shot in about the same way. You can now be thinking about the out of bounds and the topped drive as well as the short missed putt. Think of everything you can except the next stroke to be played. By your fourth stroke you will probably be in a heel print in some deep pit. This is an ideal situation for the hole-in-nine result. Curse the heel print, bawl out fate, destiny and Scotland, grip your niblick with the clutch of doom and hammer away. This should put you on the green in 6. The next few steps are easy. In place of settling down continue to boil over and rap the first putt with a savage disregard of distance or direction. This should put you about twelve feet past the cup. Your next putt will be about three feet short or over. This will be 8. The final move is to hit the ball carelessly with one hand as you pick it up and concede yourself the 9. Don't make the mistake at any time of relaxing or concentrating on the next stroke to be played. This may cut off two or more strokes.

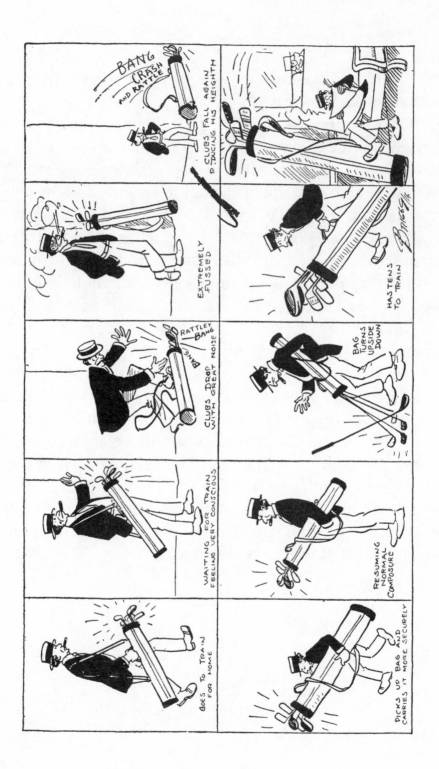

What's the Idea?

YOU can take almost any crowded golf course. And most golf courses are crowded on Saturdays and Sundays. At almost any spot on any given course you can see some player walk up to his ball. Does he take his stance comfortably, possibly waggle once or twice and then hit the ball? By no means. That would make the game too simple.

He probably stands over the ball several seconds, waggling back and forth or becoming more and more rigid. He doesn't start the back swing until his nerves are so stretched and taut and jumpy that he has to jerk the club head back.

Suppose, by some lucky chance against heavy odds, he hits a fair shot? What follows? Does he march on ahead? Not at all. He stands there like a statue carved out of granite, the club and club head gracefully draped over his left shoulder, the right heel lifted. The ball rolls on and on. Still he stands, posed against the skyline. The ball finally stops. And then reluctantly he begins to unwind and finally resume his pace. Possibly he doesn't know there are still a few golfers back of him who also would like to finish before night. Or possibly he doesn't give a whoop if there are.

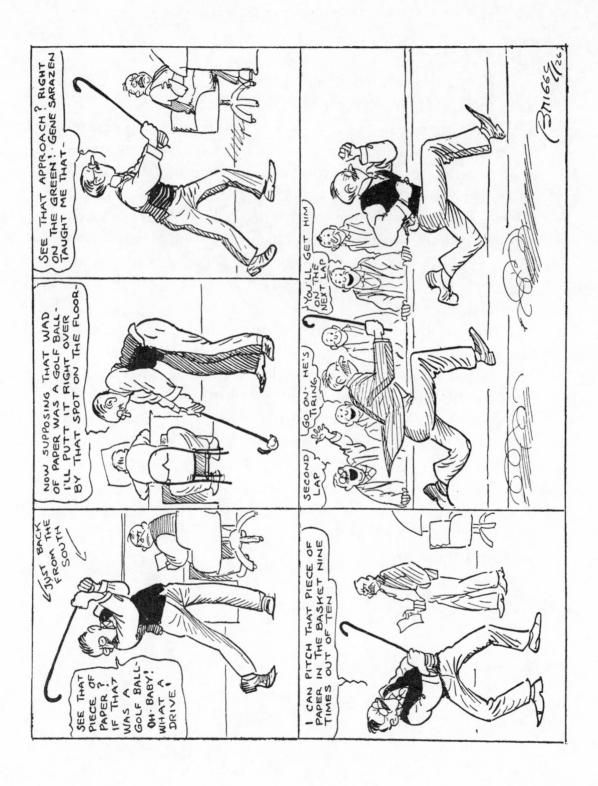

On Getting Distance

YOU stand facing a hazard which you can't carry and decide to play safe. Once in a while. Without any attempt at great effort you flick at the ball and are somewhat dazed to find you have gotten about thirty yards farther than you meant to get.

Yet there is no mystery attached. Not attempting to crowd yourself for a long carry you were carefree, relaxed and normal. Your elasticity was neither strained nor warped. You let the club head do its share of the work without attempting to hog it all. There is no violent lurch of body nor any sudden tightening of grip.

Unknowingly you have stumbled on rhythm or the secret of rhythm which in golf is simplicity of effort, unadorned with any violent exertion.

Distance is obtained by getting the club head through the ball at maximum speed. A tight grip will upset this. Hitting too soon will wreck it. Trying too hard will slow it down.

There must be the necessary amount of body turn. Don't be afraid to let the left shoulder come around. There must be balance and freedom at the top of the swing. This isn't hard to get if the head isn't moved and there is no effort at a lurch or a sway.

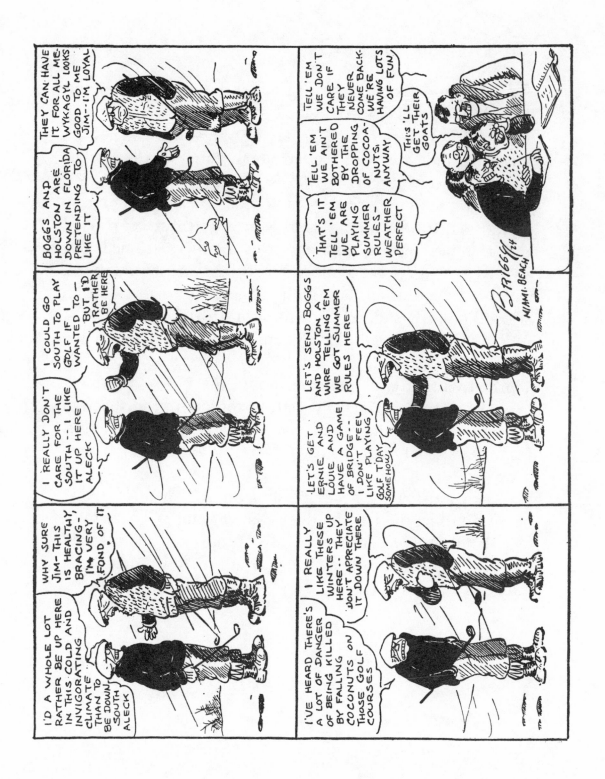

On Getting Distance

Have the feeling that you are going to apply most of your effort beyond the ball. This prevents the snap of the wrist from operating too quickly. Give the club head its chance. Get it under way and then let it keep going. You'll get the punch in soon enough without jumping to meet it.

Don't be afraid to swing through, but don't overdo it. Once the system is tightened up, all distance is done with. You are then hitting with wooden muscles in place of rubber muscles.

Swing through and let distance take care of itself. If you do, it usually will.

How to Lose Distance

"HOO-RAY! THE SHORTEST DRIVE I EVER MADE!"

NOW and then when the golfer steps upon the tee he may not feel like walking any great length after the ball. He may not be feeling well, he may have a sore heel or the day may be too warm. In that case he will want to be sure of a short drive—something from 90 to 120 yards. Strangely enough, the way to get this short drive is to adopt opposite tactics. He must say to himself—"I am going to hit this one a mile. I am going to slam the paint off this blankety-blank pill. I am going to kill it." With that thought in his mind he must then grip the club with force enough to crack a brick. This thought of extra distance and the tightened grip will send a wave of rigidity through his entire body, stiffening arms and legs, preventing a flexible pivot and breaking up all elasticity. He will be about as pliable as a pine board or a water hydrant. With every nerve and muscle in his body tense, taut and rigid he will then almost surely start a lightning back swing accompanied with a head-and-body sway. From his back swing he will lurch at the ball and apply power about two feet too soon. He will have tightened up with a snap well before the club head has reached the ball. He will have expended about 87 percent of his entire force ahead of time. As a result of all this the club head will be slowing perceptibly before the point of impact and when it reaches the ball there will be just about enough force left to get 103 yards, with fast ground and a favoring wind. It will be a serious mistake to lighten the grip, slow down the back swing, get a trifle relaxed and swing through, for in that case the golfer may have to walk 200 yards or more before he can play his next stroke.

Muscle Memory

SUPPOSE you picked up a fork and thought consciously of the right way to hold it——

Then of the correct tilt of the elbow——

And finally the proper procedure necessary to place it in your mouth.

There would at least be a fair chance of impaling your upper or lower lip, especially if you jabbed as you do with a golf club.

The fork is a simple instrument because it is operated by instinct, or muscle memory.

The golf club is almost exactly the same. You must first learn how to swing and through swinging practice make it all instinct, or muscle memory.

There must be no direct or conscious thinking about any of the details—stance, grip, pivot, elbows, wrists or body.

If you don't know the right way, the essentials at least, learn them.

If you don't want to bother with learning the right way, at least don't think about it.

It's too late to do any thinking when the club head has started by as much as an inch.

Up or Down? High or Low?

IT doesn't take any magician or three-star expert to control the trajectory of a golf ball.

There are several thousand things in life much more complex.

If you want to keep the ball low play it more off your right foot with your weight more upon your left.

If you want to get the ball up or keep it fairly high, play the ball on a line nearer your left heel and keep the weight more on your right foot.

This doesn't insure results, for you may interpolate some extra fault and throw it out of gear.

It is merely a help, the simplest way to get what you want.

The Rime of the Ancient Duffer

(Starting Coleridge One Up)

IT is an Ancient Duffer
And he stoppeth one of three;
By that long gray beard and glittering eye,
Now wherefore stoppest thou me?"

He holds him with his skinny hand,
"I had a round"—quoth he,
"Hold off—unhand me, gray-beard loon"—
Eftsoons his hands dropped he.

He holds him with his glittering eye,
The Wedding Guest stood still,
And listens like a three-year child,
The Duffer hath his will.

The Wedding Guest sat on a stone,
He cannot choose but hear;
For who is there can move an inch
When a Duffer gets your ear?

"I took three putts upon the green,
I sliced one with a spoon"—
The Wedding Guest here beat his breast
For he heard the loud bassoon.

"The traps were here—the traps where there—
The traps were all in line—
I should have had an 83—
But took a 99."

"Water, water, everywhere
For every living soul;
Water, water, everywhere
Around the nineteenth hole,
With water hazards on the side
To which my ball would roll."

"About, about, in reel and rout,
I putted for the cup;
About, about, in reel and rout,
But I was never up."

"At last I putted on a line,
And as it reached the lip,
The ball it wobbled for a spell,
And then it seemed to slip."

"With throat unslaked, with black lips baked,
I came out of the rut;
Through dull surprise all dumb I stood,
I bit my arm, I sucked the blood,
And cried—'A putt—a putt'!"

The Rime of the Ancient Duffer

"But when I got into a trap,
My caddie, with a sigh,
Quick turned his face with a ghastly pang
And cursed me with his eye."

"An orphan's curse would drag to hell
A spirit from on high;
But oh, more terrible than that,
Is the curse in a caddie's eye;
For seven holes I watched that curse,
And yet I could not fly."

"And now this spell was on—once more
I reached the rolling green;
I saw the cup—I saw the flag—
Yet stood with shaking bean"—

"Like one that on a lonesome road
Doth walk in fear and dread;
And having once turned round, walks on
And turns no more his head;

"Because he knows a frightful fiend
Doth close behind him tread;
(Deep in my heart I knew that I
Could not get that putt dead."

[81]

"I hooked—I sliced—I sliced—I hooked—
I reached twelve traps, alack;
To feel the caddie's cursing eye
Was always on my back."

"I felt it burn into my brain,
I felt it sear my soul;
I felt it when I blew each putt
Twelve inches from the hole."

"I tried the straight left arm, and then
The interlocking grip;
And then, alas, I quite forgot
To pivot at the hip."

"I held my head as Hagen does,
With open face and shut;
But what's the use of anything
If one can't hole a putt?"

"I clouted sand in bunker depths
Until my niblick blade
Was hotter than the gates of hell
Beyond the cooling shade;
And then I threw my niblick down
And clamored for a spade."

The Rime of the Ancient Duffer

"Somewhere amid that ghastly round
I hit four on a line;
I hit four but I never heard
My caddie whisper 'Fine';
I should have had an 83,
But took a 99."

The Wedding Guest sat like one stunned,
With senses all forlorn;
A sadder, but no wiser man
He rose the morrow morn,
Absorbing three hot shots of rye
And seven more of corn.

Do You Need a Willing Listener?

THE Annual Report of the Willing Ears Co. Ltd. is in full adjustment with prosperity in other lines.

You may recall the fact that the Willing Ears Co. Ltd. was formed at Belleair, Fla., several years ago by Sewell Ford and George Ade to provide Willing Listeners to golfers at normal fees or rates.

The company was formed not only to accommodate golfers in their unfettered desires to describe every shot made on any round, but also to alleviate some of the anguish and suffering that was wrecking the home, the club, the office and any other spot where a victim might be impaled by a golf nut.

Wives were beginning to break down under the strain and the help was leaving in flocks and droves.

Under the new arrangement a golfer completing a round, with a tale of terrible suffering or magnificent triumph to relate, could send for a Willing Listener and hire him by the hour. It is said that over a million wives broke into three rousing cheers when the company was formed.

In their report to the stockholders, Messrs. Ford and Ade, the leading directors, announced the largest amount of unfilled orders in the company's history.

It was something like 440,000 tons, ingots or spigots.

It has been discovered that there are now at least ten golfers to every willing listener available and this has forced an increase from the old rate of $2 an hour to $10 an hour.

It was thought at first this increase might force many golfers to skip certain unimportant details in describing their rounds, but nothing of the sort took place.

Each golfer still insisted on describing every tough break, every worm cast that wrecked a putt, every unplay-

able lie in heel print, every lucky putt his opponent holed and every brilliant putt he tapped in from four to forty feet away.

They are willing to pay almost any price for a pair of willing ears not hitched to another golfer waiting impatiently to spin his own story.

There was a heavy casualty list among the Willing Listeners, many of whom are reported to have jumped off tall buildings about the time some golfer got to a description of bunker trouble at the 13th or 14th holes.

But these ranks were easily filled at the increased rate of $10 an hour. There is a growing demand on the part of golfers for bigger and better ears, but this will cause another rate increase by the hour.

While new gushers among the golfers are being struck every day, the Company may have to grow a supply of Willing Listeners in the Philippines or South America, where large tracts have been secured.

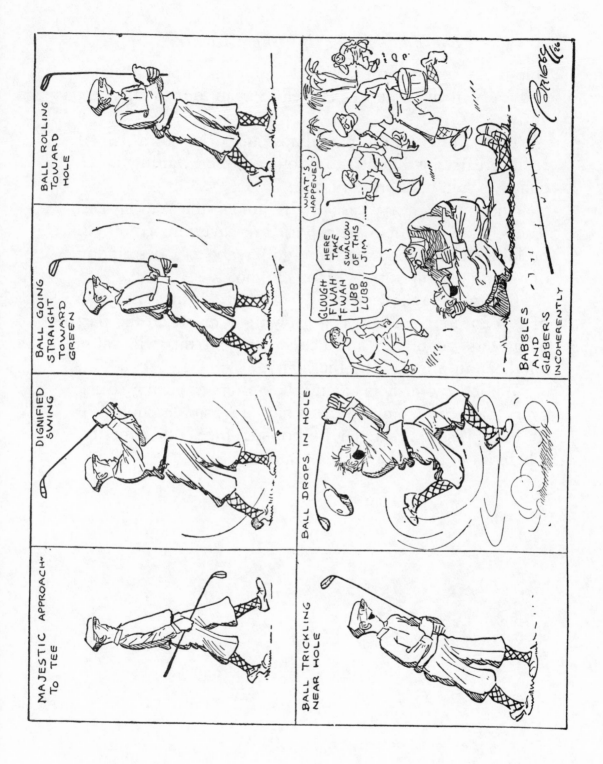

This Thing Called Rhythm

THE golf swing, of course, is nothing but a simple little
detail known as Rhythm.

That part is easy.

But in the meanwhile just what is this Rhythm the
oracles elevate to such lofty heights?

The basis of Rhythm, for the ordinary mortal, is smoothness. It is lack of violent effort. It means having everything in place at the right time.

On the back swing it is the measured, even, unhurried beat that flows like a Swinburnian lyric.

On the down swing it is the acceleration of the club head, which starts normally without a jerk or a rush and gathers speed on its way through the ball.

It is one completed piece, and not a matter of lumpy sections.

It must work of its own free will. It must not be hampered too much by thought in the act of swinging.

When the club head starts downward the main idea is to let it go upon its own roistering pace, unhurried, unchecked.

Rhythm is best expressed in any swing directed at a cigar stump or a dandelion head.

It must have firmness, lightness and increasing velocity on its way through the ball.

It starts in the brain with an oil which leaks into the muscular forces, an oil which prevents rust, creaking and any sudden snap.

The Ideal Golf Temperament

AS for the ideal golf temperament, there isn't enough of it at large to collect for laboratory purposes. Except at the rarest of intervals, it doesn't exist.

As Hek once remarked, "temperament is the highbrow word for ordinary pure cussedness." Most golfers, being temperamental at one time or another, know where they belong.

The best temperament for golf we ever saw belonged to Jerome D. Travers, Walter J. Travis and Walter Hagen. The three have won 13 national championships, match and medal, American and British. Their temperament consisted largely in thinking of just one thing while a match was in progress—viz., the next stroke to be played.

Nothing else mattered. And it doesn't. Outwardly, at least, all three have looked serene, cool and determined. Yet they have all been nervous.

Golf is played and counted stroke by stroke. A blazing soul and harsh, shrill cries of anguish won't offset the short putt you have just missed, nor the topped drive.

The ever ready alibi won't get back the fluffed mashie. Bury all the alibis in the sand of the first tee box. If you missed, you missed, and who, except yourself, cares why?

The ideal golf temperament doesn't do too much thinking in action, and its main thought is merely to hit the ball. The mental state should be a still pond, not a rushing river. In a majority of cases it is a whirlpool and a waterfall.

Decide what club you want to use, take that club and then let muscle memory do the rest as the world goes by.

There are not many who can think of one thing at a

time. There are none who can think of two or three things at the same moment.

If you don't know how to swing, it doesn't matter anyway, so far as thinking is concerned.

Fear or anger can tie any muscular system into knots. They are both enemies of rhythm. And rhythm is 92 percent of the golf swing. The hardest to beat are those who miss a short putt without blinking and who still keep on plugging.

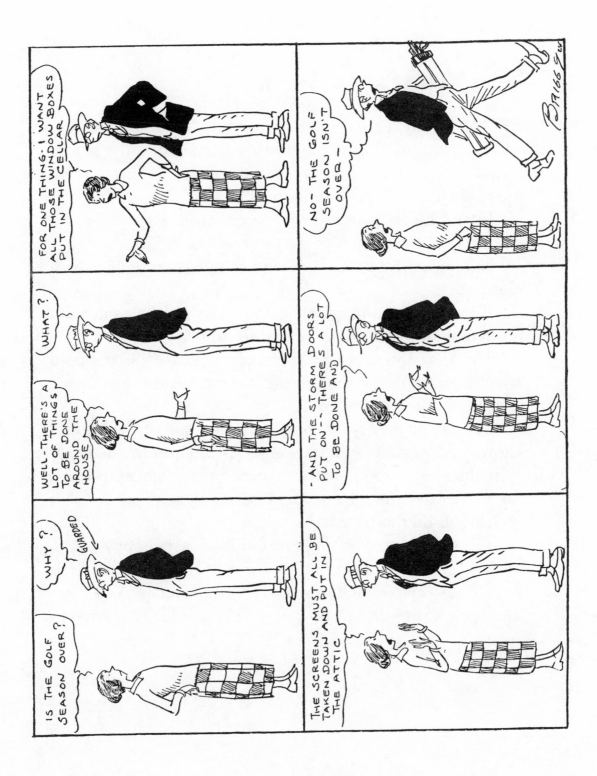

Then, There's the Spoon

THE spoon is a golf club that should be used frequently in place of a brassie and just as frequently in place of a midiron. Briefly, it is a club that should be used much more often than it is by dub and star alike.

What object is there in walking up to a close lie and seizing the brassie for a perfect top or foozle?

Not one golfer in ten thousand can play a brassie from a close lie.

Why not turn a tough shot into a fairly simple one with the spoon and gain some needed ground?

This is a habit every golfer except the few experts should adopt in full, on the spot, at the instant. Also most of the experts.

Then there comes the long iron shot, one of the hardest efforts in the game. Here again it is often much better to grip the spoon about halfway down the leather and belt the ball. It is much better because it is a safer, easier shot which will do the trick.

The spoon is one of the great clubs. Ask Bobby Jones, George Duncan, H. H. Hilton or a flock of others. It is an even greater club for the average player. And most average players don't know it. They could save enough strokes in a year to fill a freight car with this single implement.

In playing the spoon you merely stand a little closer to the ball than you do with driver or brassie and then hit or swing through the ball.

The club head's natural loft will get the ball into the air, and that's where you want it. Don't spare the shot and don't try to slug it. If it isn't a full spoon shot, grip lower on the leather and hit through firmly. And a firm left hand and left wrist and left arm make a steadying factor for the right to hit against.

Don't overlook the spoon. It's quite a club, as clubs go.

The Down-Hill Lie

THIS is one golf problem that few golfers take seriously. They make up their minds in advance that the result is going to be a terrible smear, whatever they do.

Thereupon tainted psychology comes to the aid of nature and the subsequent event is usually depressing.

As long as down-hill lies persist on most courses, one might just as well face the problem in the right way.

The first move, for a fairly long shot, is to use a mid-iron or spoon in place of a brassie. Take out a lofted club.

Put most of the weight on the left foot, bracing with a fairly straight left leg. The right knee can be bent to fit the contour of the slope.

Being comfortably braced against falling forward, play the ball on a line midway between the two feet.

Don't try any fancy long-distance hitting.

Don't be too despondent or too rigid. Keep the feet a trifle wider apart, shorten the grip and use a more upright swing.

Here is one of the few places in golf where the hands and club head can assist in getting the ball up with something approaching a lifting movement as the ball is hit. But depend more upon the lofted face of the club. The chances are the ball will be sliced, so aim more to the left of the course.

Here, at least, are a few moves in the right direction. They may not help, but it can't be much worse.

The Most Depressing Moment

CHARTING the depressing moments in golf is something like numbering the wheat blades that may cover a square mile.

There are many times when golf is nothing except one depressing moment after another. There are times when biting iron spikes in two is the only known emotional outlet.

Topping the drive on the first tee—pitching the first approach into a bunker—looking up on a chip shot for a sordid fluff—blowing a short putt of some 22 inches—pitching into a pond—no one of these episodes was ever intended to flood the heart with sunshine and starlight.

Yet the most depressing moment of all is not one of the above.

It happens when you have been slicing steadily, surely and consistently. To such an extent that you aim for the left of the course in order to hold the fairway near the extreme right.

You watch the ball skim the leaves or trees to the left, slide safely away and then finally wind up just short of the rough on the other side.

Once again you aim for the trees along the left side and wham away.

Then a horrible thing happens. In place of the expected

slice you have somehow suddenly come upon a wide hook or pull and the ball is last seen traveling out of bounds deep into the forest primeval.

It is at this moment that the shattered soul goes into more and larger convulsions than it has ever known before.

This is undoubtedly the peak.

The Golf Ball's Revenge

THE duffer cracks me on the bean,
  He leaves a big dent in my side;
O boy, I'll say he treats me mean
  By lifting chunks out of my hide.
He lands with such prodigious blows
  He has me bleeding at the nose.

And then with all his brutal force
  He swings again—at least he tries—
And hammers me clean off the course
  Into a trap that I despise;
I land half-buried, sick and blue;
  I hate sand in my mouth—don't you?

The pond comes next—with sullen frown
  He mauls me with a vicious clout;
And then I sink, and almost drown
  Before the caddie hauls me out;
I get no mercy there from him
  Although he knows that I can't swim.

He drives me into rocks and weeds,
  To swamps and rivers and to lakes,
He cuts my head until it bleeds,
  Then curses me for his mistakes;

[104]

The Golf Ball's Revenge

Sometimes his ravings get so wild
   I quiver like a beaten child.

But I get square with him at last,
   Just as he thinks—"I'll be one up"!
I see his bending shadow cast
   Where I lie two feet from the cup.
He starts me on my last short trip—
   And then—I hang upon the lip!

Still hanging in the young spring air
   I sink my teeth into the turf,
And listen as I hear him swear,
   Far wilder than the storm-swept surf;
And while he shakes his fists at me
   I sit upon the rim in glee.

"DOGGONE IF THIS ISN'T PERFECTLY DELIGHTFUL"
THIS IS THE LOVLIEST SPOT I EVER DID SEE"
" I AM GLAD TO BE ALIVE AND HAPPY"
"EVERYTHING IS SIMPLY PERFECT"
" HOORAY! I CAN TEE UP THE OLD PILL!"
" IF LIFE WAS ONLY LIKE THIS ALWAYS! WHAT HAPPINESS!"
"WELL OF ALL THE—"
" WELL I'M A — WHAT IN — — - - !?"
BRIGGS

The Only Worth-While Tip

NOW," said the friendly pro., "I want you to help Mr. A. on this round and correct some of his faults."

"I'd appreciate it," said Mr. A.

On the first tee Mr. A. hurried his back swing, lifted his head and topped the drive.

"You hurried your back swing that time and lifted your head," we suggested.

"No," replied Mr. A., "it wasn't that. I had my right hand over too far."

On the next effort Mr. A. dipped the right shoulder about 18 inches and dug up a chunk of ground back of the ball. Another fluff.

"You dipped your right shoulder that time," we suggested.

"Nothing of the kind," responded Mr. A. "I lifted my head."

On the next attempt Mr. A. made about 12 yards on a well-topped slice that limped along the turf.

A brief silence followed. "What was the trouble that time?" he asked.

"No trouble at all," we replied. "It was practically perfect."

Which is what we should have said in the first place.

The Bitter Choice

THE black spot in the average golfer's life, and this goes for those in the low 80's, comes when there is a short pitch of 50 or 75 yards to be played with a trap in front of the green and another yawning abyss waiting at the rear.

This must be rated as one of the hardest of all golf shots, for star and duffer alike, the stroke most often missed.

Just a trifle too soft and the ball plunks into the sand short of the green.

Just a trifle too hard and the ball flops into the sanded cavern beyond.

And there is usually a queer psychological action which takes place at this depressing moment.

It is about this:

The golfer at first thought makes up his mind to clear the first trap, whatever happens.

With this gallant idea in view the club head is taken back just a trifle too far and as the down swing starts the harassed player suddenly decides he is hitting much too hard. So he promptly eases up the stroke and the ball drops into the first bunker, after all.

This is the usual procedure.

In playing this shorter pitch it is much safer to take a

more lofted club, to grip nearer the bottom of the leather and to hit firmly.

All fluttering duck fits of thought must be eliminated or the head will never stay down. The body should turn but slightly and the left wrist should not be broken too quickly.

And above all here is one stroke that should not be rushed or hurried.

It is a great shot to practice until confidence comes, since confidence is the foundation of this baffling pitch to a spot between two batches of trouble.

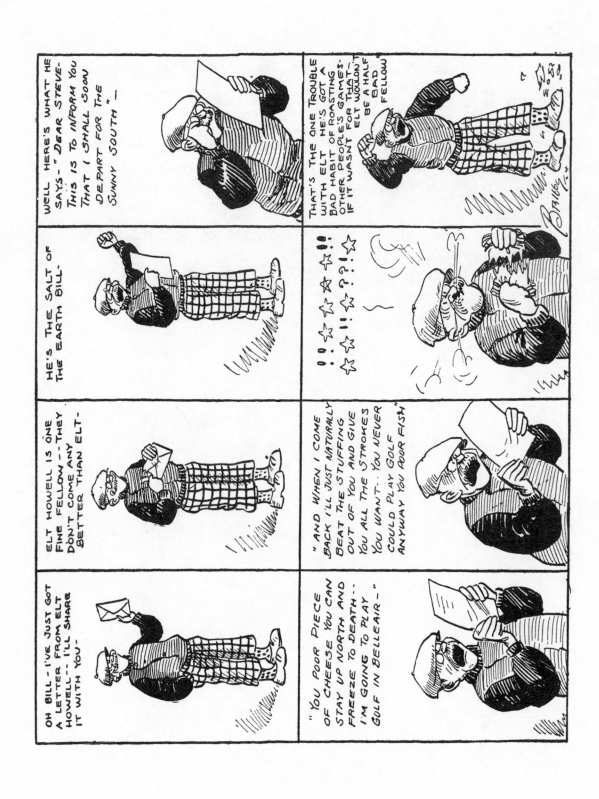

The Home Wrecker

MANY reasons have been advanced for Nero's disposition. In the same way many causes have been advanced in attempts to explain why Henry VIII murdered so many of his wives.

Yet it is all simple enough.

They both developed a bad case of "shanking" or "heeling" a mashie shot. Here is the great home wrecker of golf, the black plague of the venerable pastime.

You expect to see the ball start straight for the green when suddenly it flies off at right angles as a living pain shoots through the center of your heart. For now all confidence in your game is gone and every approach you make for days or for weeks may fly in the same direction.

J. H. Taylor, greatest of all mashie players, suffered this "heeling" disease for a year before the "heeling" could be healed.

The disease is caused by hitting the ball in the heel of the club blade, usually with the hands in advance of the swing.

It may be caused by falling forward as you swing. It may be caused by not breaking the wrists. Or possibly through bad pivoting or over-reaching. But when it arrives

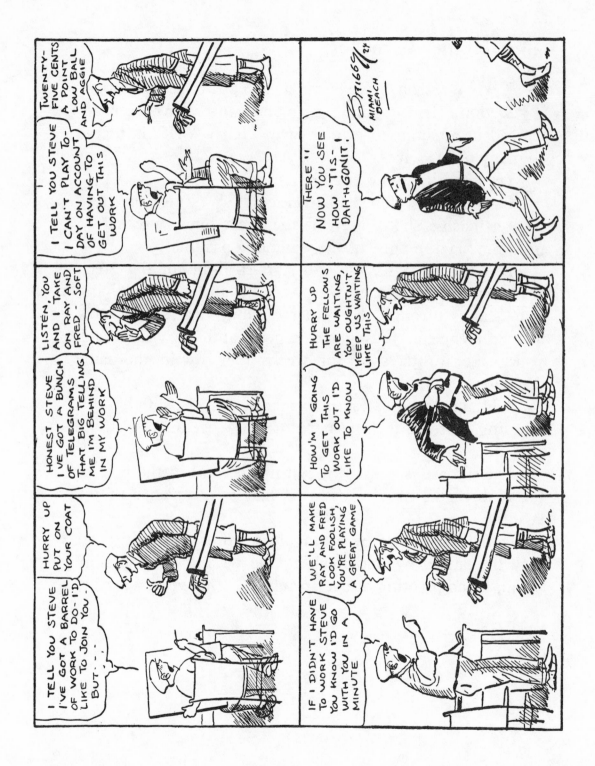

it comes with a blast that blights all hope and withers all dreams.

The best way to correct "shanking" or "heeling" is to keep the weight well back on the heels and to let the wrists break naturally at the top of the swing.

Don't make the mistake of standing farther away from the ball. If anything get a trifle closer where you can hit comfortably with the weight more on your heels.

Keep a firm left wrist to hit against so that both hands don't fly on through.

Don't be afraid to turn in the left side, without swaying forward.

This may be of some assistance. If it isn't, the only two things left are to find a good teacher in a hurry or jump from the top of the tallest building you can find.

Caddie Cantos

I SHOT a golf ball into the air;
It fell to earth, I know not where;
For when I peered by bush and lawn,
I only saw my caddie yawn.

Caddie Cantos

Blessings on thee, little man,
Barefoot boy with face of tan;
Hear me as I gently call
"Where in helengon's that ball?"

There was a little man and he had a little bag
And the bag was loaded with clubs, clubs, clubs;
And once in a while his tongue would wag
But all he muttered was "Dubs, dubs, dubs."

On Kidding Yourself

"WHY," asks Prof. Walter Hagen, "should so many golfers kid themselves?"

Why, indeed? Isn't this one of the great pastimes of all existence in every known walk of life?

By "kidding yourself" Hagen means the average golfer's refusal to accept the penalty for a poor shot.

If he hooks or slices back of a tree he will try to play some miracle recovery instead of chipping safely into the open and losing a stroke.

[118]

If he tops a drive he will attempt some impossible carry to make it up.

If he faces a trap or a pit he will try some desperate recovery that may still reach the green.

About 99 golfers out of 99 will never say—"Well, I've lost a stroke. I deserve to be penalized. I'll take the penalty. I'll play this one for the fairway."

Instead of this they stalk forth to out-Hagen Hagen or to out-Jones Jones through a miracle recovery they could never make in 17,000 years.

Whereupon they hit a tree and bound still deeper into the woods, or they still remain in the bunker after a violent lunge with a midiron and finally wind up with a 7 or an 8 in place of a 5.

When you miss a shot in golf you are supposed to lose a stroke. That's the average law of the game. The best way to get it back is to reach the fairway on your next effort and then either get an approach close to the pin or else sink a tidy putt. Your attempted "miracle recovery" will cost you just twice as many strokes as it saves. Plus a good many more. Don't try to duck all the penalties. That's what the pits, traps, bunkers, ponds, trees, lakes, rough, rivers, thickets, bushes and ditches were put there for.

In other words, as Prof. Hagen says, "Don't kid yourself."

[119]

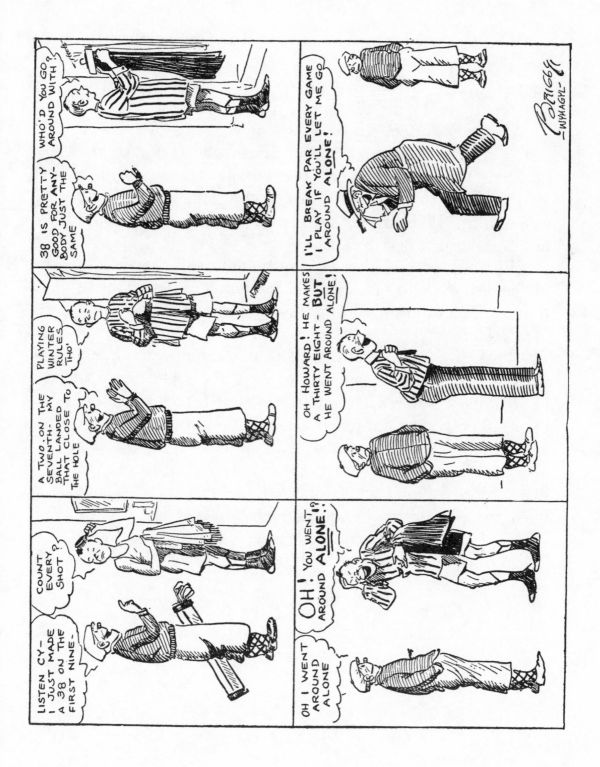

Playing the Pitch

IT would be easy enough to outline 117 different things that should be done in playing a pitch shot, but most of them would be unimportant and more of them would be forgotten.

As a starting gesture keep your body firm, your elbows fairly close and don't stand too far away from the ball.

Keep a firm left hand and a firm left wrist, broken slightly at the top of the swing, but after all it is mainly a right-hand swing and a right-hand hit.

Keep your weight a trifle more on the right foot than the left.

Now you come to the more important part. Make up your mind decisively how hard you want to hit the ball— and then hit it without quitting on the stroke.

And don't be in a hurry to get it over. Keep your back swing smooth and unrushed, and finish your back swing before you hit through. You can even pause or hesitate a half second at the top of the swing. Or three-quarters of a second. Or just a brief interval.

Don't be afraid to hit firmly, cutting the grass from under the ball without digging for the turf.

And don't try to lift the ball with club head or hands. That's why they built clubs with lofted blades. For short pitches use well-lofted clubs so you can hit firmly; for not one golfer in nine thousand can spare or soften a pitch.

For the longer pitch there should be a "feel" or "pull" at the left shoulder as it turns in. Sorry there's no more descriptive term. But the left shoulder has some influence on this stroke, as well as the right hand hitting through. It helps to guide or to steady the punch. And keep your weight back more than forward.

This is quite enough to think about for the time being.

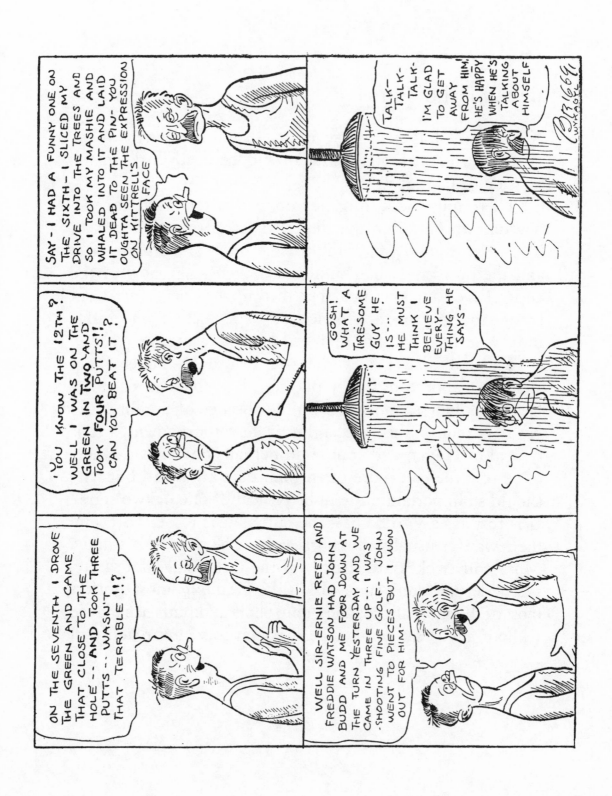

Beyond the Pin

WHAT dragons are waiting beyond the pin? What gorillas, ghosts, cobras or sudden death lurk on the far side of the cup?

There must be killing horror in that territory since so few dare to play into that deserted territory. You can sit by any green and watch the mashie pitches, the chip shots and the putts and about nine out of ten stop short of the cup. It is a curious fact that the cup has never yet been known to come forward to meet the ball. Yet not one golfer in fifty makes a habit of giving the ball a chance.

The ball that passes the pin is usually better hit— straighter and more firmly played. It is the sign of stout-hearted boldness, adorned with the absence of timidity, and yet it is one of the rare sights in any tournament. It is typical of Hagen and Jones and perhaps one or two others to be past the cup more often than they are short, but why should so important an item be typical of one or two stars? It is just as easy to be past the cup as it is to be short, and the reward is usually much greater. The answer is simple. Most golf strokes are struck on the timid side, the safety-first side, the don't-run-a-risk side. Among most golfers most of the short approaches, chip shots and putts are played without any great confidence. The average approach putt

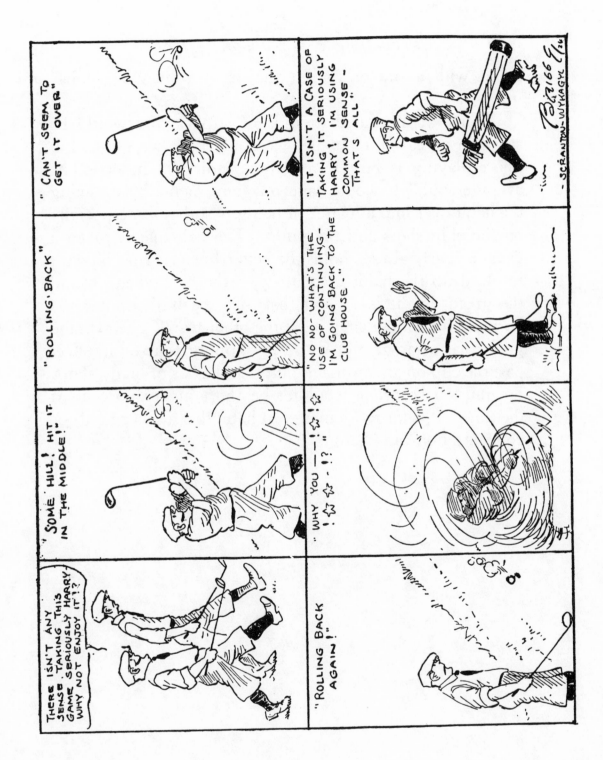

is hit with a prayer that it may stop somewhere fairly near.

Think of all the thousands of strokes that would be saved in a year if 18 inches were added to every putt hit. Short playing is largely a mental habit which seizes the average soul. It would take no giant mentality to swing the habit over into a matter of being past the pin, especially on the chip shots and the putts. The ball that is given a chance nearly always holds the better line. It isn't difficult to build up the habit of being past the cup when around the green, but it is a habit that must be built up for the normal human tendency is all the other way. The average golfer has a far greater dread of slipping four or five feet past the cup on an approach putt than he has of being short. He must have or he wouldn't be short ninety percent of the time. It is largely a matter of habit that a few rounds of concentration can change.

The Useful Loft

"EACH man to his taste," as the Chinaman said who devoured a rodent. And the taste of this author is not in favor of too much loft on mashies and mashie niblicks.

A niblick with the blade laid well back is a necessary implement.

But a mashie niblick for the average golfer, one of the most useful of all clubs, should have only a trifle more loft than a mashie.

The blade should be fairly expansive with a comfortable amount of loft and when that happens the club is easy to play, one of the easiest in the whole kit of tools.

In playing the mashie niblick the ball should be fairly close in and so should the elbows.

Keep the weight just a bit more on the heels and then thump for the pin.

If the shot doesn't pan out you have probably fallen forward, hurried the swing, lifted your head or dipped the right shoulder. Any one of these is fatal.

The Duffer's Requiem

(With due apologies to Robert Louis Stevenson)

UNDER the wide and starry sky
   Dig the grave and let me lie;
Gladly I've lived and gladly die
Far from this world of strife.

These be the lines you grave for me—
"Here he lies where he wants to be;
Here he lies by the Nineteenth Tee,
Where he's lied all through his life."

Famous or Favorite Clubs

JOCK HUTCHISON'S most famous club was known as a "stopum."

B. L. T. once charged Percy Hammond with having only three clubs in his bag, a "topum," "loseum" and a "wet-um."

Few golfers ever start a round without a "foozle-um" and they rarely ever finish without a "tell-um."

The "tell-um" is by all odds the golfer's favorite weapon.

In this stroke the tongue is pivoted back and forth as long as the listener will remain in reach.

No back spin is ever used. It is all follow through.

A Tip from Walter Hagen

(Who has won both United States and British Open
Championships Twice)

ALMOST every golfer, good, bad or indifferent, is pretty sure to spend a certain part of his time in trouble.

So the main problem of golf is how to get out of trouble with as little stroke loss as possible.

The greatest difference between the star and the average player is the way they handle bunkers, pits or the rough.

Part of this is mental. Most of it is. The star knows he is pretty sure to get out in one stroke, so he doesn't worry much.

The duffer doesn't know how long he may be in the pit or trap.

As a result the star takes a natural grip, doesn't tighten too much, doesn't hurry the stroke and lets fly with confidence.

My tip to the average golfer in trouble is not to grip so tightly, not to take it so much as a life-and-death matter, and get more play in the wrists.

The hands and wrists are the main devices for getting the ball out of trouble. So don't let them get too stiff or too rigid. Don't squeeze the leather until hand and wrists are like pieces of wood. Keep them normal and let some of the elastic stuff remain. Just remember that.

How to Top a Mashie Shot

QUITE often on a spring morning or a summer's afternoon the golfer feels a burning desire to top his mashie shot while approaching one of the best trapped holes on the course. There are few things in life or nature more beautiful than the sight of a well-topped approach skimming along the grass as the ball slips swiftly over the green into some deep pit just beyond.

If the urge becomes extreme there are several ways to insure this topping result. The surest way is to try to lift the ball with the blade of the mashie in place of hitting straight through with a firm left wrist. Let the hands lift the mashie blade just as it reaches the ball with the left wrist somewhat flabby. There is no finer way to top. There is no surer way. If the left wrist is held firm as the right hand hits through and under the ball, a pitch may result in place of a fast flying topped target on its way to a bunker.

Another sound method of topping is to take a natural stance and then straighten up just as one starts the back swing. In this way the hands are lifted and kept well up in place of being kept down through the swing.

Topping a golf ball is no insignificant art. If the wrists are kept quite rigid with almost no touch of flexibility, one is sure to be upon the right road, provided the right road

[133]

is along the ground and not up in the air. Undoubtedly the simplest of all topping systems is to attempt to lift the ball with the hands and club head. No one yet has found any improvement upon this direct method of keeping the bounding ball along the turf.

The Swinburnian Golfer

FROM too much bunker living,
From tops and hooks set free,
I thank, with brief thanksgiving
What golfing gods there be
That no slice is forever,
That good putts hop out never,
And that the star most clever
Can top one from the tee.

From dubs who tell dull stories
Of holes they made in par;
From pests who shout the glories
Of drives that carried far,
I thank all exits near me,
Or portals that will clear me,
Or taxis that will steer me
To some well-hidden bar.

A Few Words on the Mashie

THE mashie, it might just as well be stated now as later, is not a meat axe. Neither is it a shovel. It was not invented to cut gashes in the ball, nor to dig holes in the ground. Its primary purpose is to get the ball well into the air and keep it there until the ball can drop on some green. It was not intended for a high, short pitch nor for a wallop of 150 or 160 yards. The mashie niblick and the mashie iron or midiron can look after these jobs. The mashie is a club to be used with ease, comfort and confidence. It is not to be over-swung. It calls for firm wrists with a slight break or bend in the left at the top of the swing. It calls for a firm body, turning only moderately, and for an unmoved headpiece. A firm left wrist is essential, so the right hand and wrist can have something to snap against without any sudden lifting. The back swing can be restricted. But the down swing should never be spared or checked or shackled. There should be no sudden tightening on the down swing, as this slows down the speed of the club head.

The mashie hates to reach for a ball. It prefers a ball closer to the feet where the flying elbows can be restrained and where the swing can be kept compact. It prefers to be taken back smoothly and evenly with a slight pause at the top. On the down swing its object is to cut the grass out from under the ball without digging a hole or without being lifted by the hands. But always it demands that this down swing be firm and free, never softened or throttled.

The left shoulder should be the main hinge for the mashie shot, with a firm left wrist acting almost as if it were part of the shaft through most of the back swing. The mashie hates flabbiness and hurry and it doesn't like to be forced. Neither does it like to be spared. All it demands is a natural effort.

25 Tips from James M. Barnes

(Who has won both United States and British Open
Championship)

Here are the twenty-five best tips I can offer in concentrated form:

1. Take a stance that is easy and natural, with the knees slightly and comfortably bent.

2. Keep your feet comfortably well apart on full shots, but closer together as you approach the green.

3. Be sure that your grip is not too tight, just a trifle firmer in the left hand than in the right.

4. Let the left hand take main control of the back swing —in no case lifting the club away from the ball with the right.

5. Be sure that the club head starts back evenly, and not with a hurried jerk or lift.

6. Be sure that the club head starts back on an arc inside of the ball, and is not lifted outside of the ball.

7. Keep the left arm straight, but not stiff or rigid.

8. Don't think of the wrists—let them turn naturally at the top of the swing.

9. Be sure to hold the head as an anchor, letting the body turn or pivot in the same space without swaying.

10. As the left shoulder starts around let the left knee turn in naturally toward the ball.

11. Keep the right elbow fairly close to the body, not letting it lift too high.

12. At the top of the swing see that the weight is on the right leg and right foot and on the inside ball of the left foot to get balance.

13. On the down swing be sure that the two hands, starting the club, don't get too far in front of the club head.

14. On the down swing be sure that the body doesn't get in ahead of the arms, but follows in a natural way.

15. At the moment of impact, as the club head crashes into the ball, be sure the left leg is firmly braced to meet the shock and hold the body in place.

16. In mashie play keep the ball in closer to the feet, where the forehead is over the ball. Don't stand too far away.

17. For a chip shot let the left hand steady the club, with the right hand doing most of the work.

18. If you are missing short putts, try gripping less tightly.

19. To slice, keep the left foot farther back and use a more upright swing.

20. To pull, advance the left foot and swing more in a flatter arc.

[141]

21. Make up your mind in advance what you intend to do, the line you want, how hard you are to hit.

22. With your mind made up, as you take your stance, think on through the stroke—or don't think at all.

23. Don't try to keep your eye on the ball—keep your mind on it—and not on some bunker or pond on ahead.

24. Never get careless, but don't concentrate too much. Keep the mind relaxed and the muscles will follow this lead.

25. In heavy grass or in sand, don't grip too tightly and lunge at the ball. Stick more than ever to a firm, natural effort.

A Chant of the Kiplingesque

BY a bunker down in Dixie, where the Gulf Stream
cleaves the sea,
There's a mashie shot awaiting, and I know it thinks of me;
For the wind is in the palm trees and the sundrifts seem to
say:
"Come you South, you bally duffer, come you South to loaf
and play."

The dreamy winds are singing where the pine trees sway
and croon,
And a silver moon is shining just the same as it was June;
And the mashie niblick's whirring in the sand traps and
the ruts
Where a line of sun-baked duffers keep a-missing of their
putts.

I am sick of wasting leather where the snow is on the green,
And this blasted Northern drizzle leaves a burning in my
bean;
Though I talk with fifty experts where the snow has left a
wreck,
I had rather miss one brassie where the sun is on my neck.

A Chant of the Kiplingesque

Ship me somewhere south of Dixie, where a cove can swing
    a cleek,
Where the ten-foot putts are dropping and the fairway's
    green and sleek:
For the mashie shots are calling, and it's there that I
    would be,
Where I'm six up on some duffer as we leave the seventh tee.

Ship me somewhere south of Dixie, where the skyline's pink
    and blue,
Where the low winds cross the palm belt and I reach the
    green in two;
Where I hear the inland echoes or I watch the rolling surf,
As the mashie blade goes tearing for its grip with Southern
    turf.

You can have your Northern winters, but I'll take the palms
    for mine,
The whisper through the maple and the music of the pine;
Better fifty days of sunshine with a midiron and the rose,
Better fifty days in bunkers than a cycle in the snows.

Off the Edge of the Green

THE chip shot from some spot just off the green is frequently easier than the long-approach putt.

In fact it nearly always is.

It is one of the simplest of all the golfing charades.

Keep your feet fairly close together and stand reasonably close to the ball. It is mainly a right-hand and right-arm movement.

"Take the club back with the right-hand and arm," advises Jim Barnes, "and merely use the left for greater steadiness. A firm left hand and left wrist are necessary."

"Keep the body still," advises Barnes, "with only a slight turn of the left knee. Keep both elbows compact and use a shorter grip on mashie iron, mid mashie or jigger, the best types for this stroke."

You can even have the feeling of holding the club head down with the left so that it can't be lifted too quickly as the right hand "pinches" the ball away from the ground.

Don't be afraid to stand pretty well over the ball and don't be afraid to hit it up to the cup or pin.

Above everything else don't hurry the club head back or hurry it through. The chip shot should be as smooth as the putt, flowing like a steady stream. If it isn't smooth, even, steady and unhurried it won't work. That's one tip on which you can bet your ultimate kopeck or your final ruble.

[147]

Getting Out of the Sand

GOOD bunker play is largely a matter of mind over matter. "Mind," relates Don Marquis, "is superior to matter—when there's nothing the matter."

That's where the rub enters. When you are in a bunker or a trap it often matters a great deal.

In playing from the sand there are just a few details that are highly important, unless you like the sand better than the fairway.

Getting Out of the Sand

The first move is to get the feet firmly planted and to keep the body as relaxed as possible.

This "jousting in the sand-filled trough" calls for more flexibility than stiffness.

If you are exploding the ball out, always the safest method, pick out a spot just back of the ball—ordinarily about an inch back—and hit down through that spot under the ball. You lift as the sand is reached.

You will have a much better chance to emerge if you lighten your grip to give the wrists their chance and don't hurry the blow.

There is only a slight turn of the body on this shot, and don't stop the club head in the sand. Let it gouge its way on through.

Most golfers enter a bunker taut with desperation and stiffened by despair. The usual mistake is to dig too far back of the ball, dropping the right shoulder as they swing down.

Bunker play must be orderly and unhurried, backed up by mental poise.

Those who surrender as they peer into the depths are licked in advance.

After all it is part of the game and one of its most important and most exciting moments.

Stand back of the ball, not too far away, and use a more

upright swing where the hands and arms do the work— not the body.

Don't be afraid of the shot. Slash through with abandon and enthusiasm, defying fate and gravity. The main idea is to reach the open again and not to be too fancy.

On Remaining in a Bunker

THERE are thousands of golfers to whom the bunker is home. There are thousands who spend more time in one bunker or another than they ever think of spending by their firesides. The fairway is strange country where they feel horribly ill at ease and out of place. They seem to like the bunkers better than the fairways because they spend so much more time in the former. They will frequently get into the first bunkers in sight and hardly miss one around the course. It is like Old Home Week when they reach the sand.

It is no great trick to hit the ball into a bunker. It is no great trick to stay there. Yet there are a few valuable hints that might be followed. The best way to remain indefinitely in a bunker is to enter the sand with a feeling of despondency, bordering on wrath. Make no attempt to get the feet settled well into the sand. Then grip the niblick as if it were a battleaxe. Lunge back swiftly and then lunge forward without picking out any spot just back of the ball. The idea is to hammer blindly away with the wrists stiff and rigid.

Another sure way of remaining indefinitely in the sand-filled trough is to attempt to flick the ball out cleanly, barely touching the sand with the blade of the club. About four such attempts will frequently advance the ball eight or ten inches. It is a mistake for those desiring to spend more time in the abyss to get the feet set properly, to keep the wrists flexible, to pick out a spot just back of the ball and not hurry the stroke. If this is done without checking the niblick blade the ball may fly out at once and thereby bring the golfer out of his native haunt ahead of the schedule.

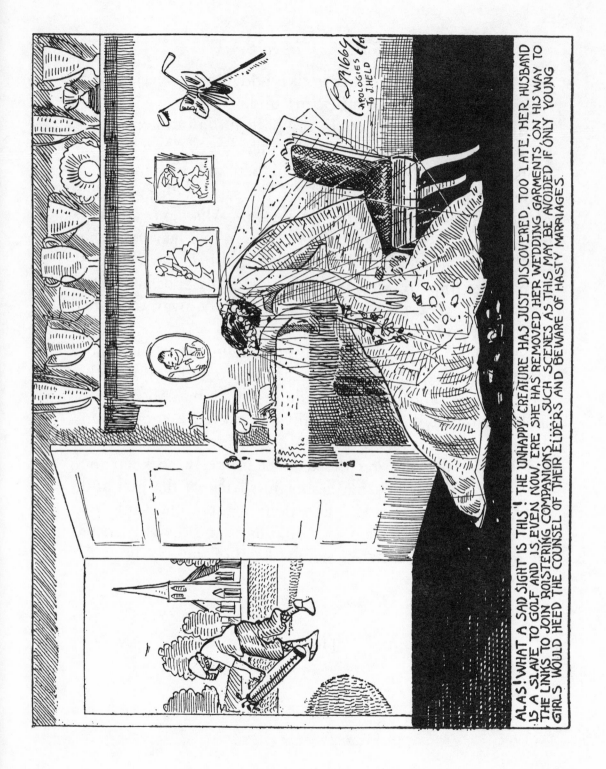

How to Take Three Putts

"DON'T YOU DARE DROP IN THAT CUP! I WANT TO PUTT YOU AGAIN"

MANY golfers enjoy putting to such an extent that they take three or four putts to the green. There are times or occasions when they will get down in one putt, possibly clean across the green, much to their disgust. For after all it is not hard to take three or even four putts to a green if one is only willing to follow a few crude suggestions.

First, in addressing the ball for the first putt, stand over it long enough to get completely rigid, if not jumpy in the nerves.

Look at the line to the hole and then try to judge the speed of the green and the distance to be covered. Think of all these details in one blurred mass as you start your back swing. Start the back swing with something approaching a swift jerk. Then stab or jab the ball without any attempt at a follow through, lifting your head and moving your body. This will leave you six or seven feet short of the cup, or five or six feet beyond. But you will probably be short. Missing the next putt is child's play. Grip the shaft of the putter as tightly as possible. Get completely rigid. Use another fast, jerky back swing and once more stab the ball as the body moves. This method is sure to leave you another putt of eighteen or twenty inches.

Be sure not to lighten the grip or to keep the head and body still. Be sure not to start the back swing evenly and smoothly without any hurry. Be sure not to stroke the ball on the way through. For in that case you will probably hole out from five or six feet and so miss the pleasure or thrill of taking another putt. You can always increase the number of your putts by increasing the speed of the putting blade and the tightness of your grip. Also by lifting your head and moving your body.

Simplified Putting

THERE have been at least 386 different suggestions offered to bring about consistent or successful putting. The average golfer has attempted to apply from 23 to 36 of these suggestions at the same time. Or he hasn't tried any suggestions or followed any plans, which is almost as bad. Yet good putting is only a matter of two simple details. If these two details are followed out the ball is certain to begin dropping with greater frequency in the bottom of the cup on distances ranging from four to ten feet.

The first simplified detail is to keep the head and body still. Comfortable and at least normally relaxed, but still.

The second detail is to stroke the ball. Only that, as the Raven muttered, and nothing more whatsoever.

If the head and body are relaxed and unmoved there will be no head lifting and no body swaying. There will be no ducking of the knee.

If the ball is stroked there will be a follow through, and this means no jabbing or stabbing. Stroking implies a normal grip, not a frenzied one, and a lack of hurry. Hagen and Jones, the two greatest putters now playing, stand differently and look different. But they both keep head and body still and they both stroke the ball. Any minor improvements to assist the operation can be tacked on later.

On Sinking the Putt

ONE might write from three thousand to twelve thousand words on the art, science or craft of putting and still leave much untold. But little of it would be digested and all of it would be forgotten.

The true art of putting embraces only a few essential ingredients which are not hard to remember.

Yet they can only be applied consistly through mental poise and nerve control.

The first act is a comfortable stance with the weight preferably on the left foot and leg to hold the body still. And this doesn't mean maybe. The head and body must not move.

The next official act is to employ a light, firm grip that is in no sense compressed or frenzied. The putting stroke belongs to the hands, wrists and forearms. The left hand leads in taking the blade back and the right hand has full control of the forward motion. The left merely helps steady the club as the right does the stroking.

The final operation is to keep the putting blade along the ground and stroke through, in place of stabbing or jabbing.

With a still body and a stroking system, putting loses most of its terror.

On Sinking the Putt

The basis of putting is smoothness, and there can be no smoothness with a fast back swing and the grip of doom. It is probably safer to take the club head back a trifle on the inside of the ball. And don't lift the club head suddenly from the ground.

On short putts it is of course much safer to use a short back swing. There is less margin for error.

On the long-approach putt the mental side is important and simple.

Pick out your line and decide on the speed of the green. Make both decisive, right or wrong. Cast out the haunting devil of doubt.

There isn't much more to be said if you will follow these suggestions and practice them at every chance. It will only be a matter of brief time before your opponents are applying all the vitriolic epithets they can think of, which is the highest compliment a deadly putter can receive.

A Tip from Bobby Jones

I BELIEVE," remarked the noted amateur, accepting the loan of a lighted match, "that golf is hard enough as it is, without being made any harder.

"For this reason I believe in simplifying the game without trying to hit low shots into the wind, high shots with the wind, or try out hooks and slices on dog-leg holes. I think it's a much safer plan just to hit the ball firmly and keep it as straight as you can without trying too many varieties. If the hook or slice comes off you are not in much better shape than you would have been by hitting a straight shot to a safer place. And if they don't come off, you are practically ruined when there are woods or water around.

"When you walk up to the ball just say to yourself this is a mashie niblick shot, a mashie shot, an iron shot, a spoon shot or whatever it is, take your stance, forget everything else and hit the ball, without trying to be too fancy about it. Even the simple shots without trying for cut, back spin, slice, hook or altitude are not always as simple as they look. But they are the easiest and the safest to play, and that is the main idea."

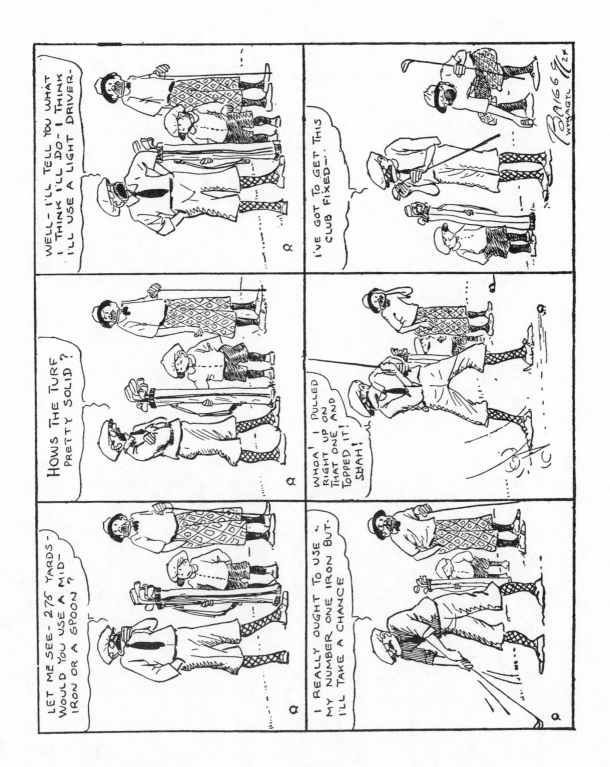

Afterword
by
Jim Murray

"Golf," a playing partner of mine is wont to explain, "is the pursuit of infinity."

My partner would love "The Duffer's Handbook of Golf."

Clubs have changed, the ball has changed, courses have changed—but Golf has not changed. The game that Grantland Rice and Clare Briggs found is the same devilish, confounding, frustrating, mocking pursuit that we find today.

Don Quixote would understand golf. It is the impossible dream, it is Dulcinea, the lovely fair maiden we see and not the slattern nobly robed only in our imagination.

It's nice to know the game doesn't get any easier. Don't worry about golf. A thing mastered is a thing scorned. Where breathes there a man so incautious as to be contemptuous of golf? Brave men tread lightly in its presence. They fear to wake up the sleeping lion.

Listen to "The Duffer's Handbook" cajole us: "The four controlling qualities (of golf) are Serenity, Determination, Relaxation and Concentration."

Hah!

The four controlling qualities are Tension, Indecision, Temerity and Insecurity.

It's comforting to know our forefathers (if 1926 can be considered to be an era of forefathers) found this blessed game to be just as vexing, just as capricious as we do. And as fascinating. They worried about where to put the "Vee's," about not having the left hand too far over on the club shaft, about keeping the right hand from controlling the shot.

Why, this book is as modern as metal woods, square grooves! "The right hand will be fairly itching to get in and take control but make it wait awhile." Now, who said that?! Granny Rice in 1926—or the leader in the clubhouse after the third round of the 1988 Masters? You think that thought didn't go through Sandy Lyle's mind as he stood on the 18th at Augusta last April?

And the Clare Briggs' cartoons! You think this man didn't suffer out on the golf course with the rest of us? You think he didn't 4-putt a green with a chance to win the money all four ways on an 18th green?

Ah, Golf! You old harlot, you! We are all like that character in Somerset Maugham's "Of Human Bondage." We are in thrall to a lady who mocks us. Yet there is nothing we wouldn't do for her. We are sure she will come to love us in time.

"Eat, drink and be merry," our author advises us. Because tomorrow you may shoot higher. "If, at first, you don't succeed, try looking at the ball."

Yes, as my friend Nick Seitz says, it is "the king of games." It rules you, not you, it. The way it should be. It is chess. Every other game is Chinese checkers.

Golf is all in the fingers, they tell us. Humbug. It's all in the mind. It's not conscience that doth make cowards of us all, it's sandtraps. Once when the baseball player, Maury Wills, was having trouble hitting the curveball, someone told him it was all in his mind. "That's the worst place to have it," Wills told him. "If it was in my leg I could have it fixed." Maury went to a hypnotist.

The duffers of the 1920s found the same public enemies on a course that we do. Public Enemy No. 1 is the slice, the dreaded right-to-right shot. There is a whole page of instructions on how to slice. This is a novel and effective approach. Far more instructive in its way than a page on how not to slice. It tells you that if you bring the club back inside you will *defeat the purpose which is to slice the ball. You may hook or, alack! you may even hit a straight ball. If you develop a sway, it tells you, what you must do is then aim directly for the rough on the right.*

"The Duffer's Handbook" talks of "mashies" and "niblicks" but the implements don't matter. Golf towers above the puny implements manufactured for its mastery. Graphite shafts, aluminum shafts, metal-wood heads, fibre-glass, square grooves, golf is not to be brought low by metallurgy or toolmaking or cabinetry. It knows you won't keep your head still.

The golf course is the last stand of the torture chamber in this century. It is a game invented by Torquemada. It is the Devil's Island of Sport. I love every perverse blade of grass, every hanging lie, four-break green, and blind carry in it. So did Clare Briggs and Grantland Rice. Their love shines through every complaining chapter from "How To Make A Hole in 9" to "How To Lose Distance." Unrequited love makes the best reading. Any tabloid editor can tell you that. If you will ever show me a person whose love golf requites—well, you'll ruin my afternoon.

Jim Murray